5/07

OMNIBUS PRESS PRESENTS THE STORY OF
Gwen Stefani

BY AMY H. BLANKSTEIN

D1573256

RAWN

OMNIBUS PRESS
LONDON · NEW YORK · SYDNEY

OMNIBUS PRESS
LONDON · NEW YORK · SYDNEY

Picture research, cover and book design by Sarah Nesenjuk
ISBN 0-8256-3438-5
Order No. OP 51249

Exclusive Distributors:

Music Sales Corporation

257 Park Avenue South, New York, NY 10010 USA

Music Sales Limited

8/9 Frith Street, London W1D 3JB United Kingdom

Music Sales Pty. Limited

120 Rothschild Street, Rosebery, Sydney, NSW 2018 Australia

Photo Credits:

Front Cover: **Sven Hoogerhuis**/LFI

Back Cover: **David Fisher**/LFI

Evan Agostini/Getty: 4 & 98. **Ron Akiyama**/Frank White: 3, 51, 83 & 101. **Sebastian Artz**/Getty: 22. **Aura**/Getty: 81. **Dave Benett**/Getty: 30. **Vince Bucci**/Getty: 32 & 96. **Cyberimage**/LFI: 49r. **Anthony Dixon**/LFI: 6. **Fox**/Getty: 56. **Getty**/Getty: 57. **Scott Gries**/Getty: 68. **Bryan Haraway**/Getty: 49l. **Scott Harrison**/Getty: 70. **Kathryn Indiek**/LFI: 93. **Gie Knaeps**/LFI: 52. **Marc Larkin**/LFI: 13. **Jen Lowery**/LFI: 42, 45, 50, 54 & 63. **Arnaldo Magnani**/Getty: 34. **Mark Mainz**/Getty: 78. **Kevin Mazur**/LFI Images: 53b. **Frank Micelotta**/Getty: 26, 35, 67 & 94. **Tim Mosenfelder**/Getty: 10, 18, 20, 60 & 102. **Liam Nicholls**/Getty: 41. **Lucy Nicholson**/Getty: 74. **Patti Ouderkirk**/Frank White: 9, 17, 28 & 46. **Derek Ridgers**/LFI: 29. **Eric Ryan**/Getty: 87. **John Rogers**/Getty: 100. **Joy E. Scheller**/LFI: 15. **Myrna Suarez**/Getty: 86 & 90. **Alberto Tamargo**/Getty: 58 & 73. **Frank White**: 24, 38 & 104. **Michael Williams**/LFI: 64 & 84. **Kevin Winter**/Getty: 8, 49b, 53r, 53l & 75.

Printed in the United States of America

Visit Omnibus Press at www.musicroom.com

Introduction

In 1987, three friends from Anaheim, California—John Spence, Eric Stefani, and his reluctant sister, Gwen—decided to form the ska band, No Doubt. After Spence's tragic death and Eric's departure to pursue a career in animation, Gwen was the only one of the original three No Doubt members who would remain. No Doubt, which coalesced early on into a core line up of Gwen, Tony Kanal, Tom Dumont, and Adrian Young, quickly captured a strong following in southern California with its unique blend of ska, new wave, and punk, but struggled for years to gain recognition beyond the regional touring circuit.

Nearly ten years after its formation, No Doubt exploded onto the mainstream music scene with its third LP, *Tragic Kingdom*. Hard on the heels of the release of the album's first single, "Just A Girl," in 1995, No Doubt became an "overnight" sensation, which propelled singer Stefani into the limelight. Despite the tensions within the band caused by the media focus on Gwen, the band rallied to capitalize on *Tragic Kingdom's* popularity with lots of touring and strong follow-up albums such as *Return of Saturn* and *Rock Steady*.

Fast forward to 2005, No Doubt boasts multiple multi-Platinum selling albums and international stardom, and Gwen—who had to be coaxed by her brother to join—has become a star in her own right. In 2003, Stefani—who has designed her own clothes since she was young and whose fashion whims are followed by music fans and fashionistas alike—launched her own clothing and accessories line. And in 2004, Stefani nabbed her first major motion picture role, portraying Jean Harlow opposite Leonardo Di Caprio in Martin Scorsese's film, *The Aviator*.

Coming off the success of *Rock Steady* and with so many side projects in motion, it would have been understandable if Stefani took a breather while No Doubt took a hiatus. Instead, with the release of her 2004 album, *Love.Angel.Music.Baby.*, Stefani took the opportunity to explore new musical territory as a solo artist. *Love.Angel.Music.Baby.* is a departure from No Doubt's signature sound. Conceived as a lark with bandmate Tony Kanal, its tracks are pure retro '80s dance music. The album, produced in collaboration with a host of top-tier collaborators, took on a life of its own, and to date has spawned four chart-topping singles.

Nearly two decades after she hit the stage, it's safe to say that Stefani has achieved pop icon status, but what is it about Gwen Stefani that makes her *Gwen Stefani, pop icon?* Like the lead character in her favorite musical, *The Sound of Music,* it's hard to pin her down.

Her appeal crosses many lines. Guys think she's sexy because of her platinum-haired good looks, bared midriff, and washboard abs. Girls want to be her: She's independent, creative, successful, confident, goofy, and glamorous, and strongly embraces being a girlie girl—and lest we forget, is married to fellow rocker and heartthrob, Gavin Rossdale of Bush and Institute fame. Fans love her because she's wild and energetic on stage. The fashion world loves her because of her unique and playful sense of style. Other stars like her because she's humble and easy to work with. She's warm, friendly, hard working, humble, self deprecating, and unaffected. She's Betty Boop, Dorothy of Oz, Jean Harlow, Betty Grable, Marilyn Monroe, Madonna, Cyndi Lauper, Pat Benatar, and Debbie Harry rolled into one.

But perhaps it's best to leave it to her fans to answer that question. "When I think of Gwen I think of individuality," one young female fan told the *Sacramento Bee* in June 2004. "I love that she can do what she does. Making a solo CD, doing a clothing line. She embraces who she is and where she came from. It makes me want to embrace my nerdy side."

No doubt Stefani, who to this day insists that, underneath it all, she is a nerd, would agree.

CHAPTER ONE

Just A Girl

Gwendolyn Renée Stefani was born on October 3,1969, just fourteen years after Walt Disney opened the Disneyland theme park in her hometown of Anaheim, California. Walt, whose company still sells the fantasy of family-oriented entertainment, would likely have approved of her upbringing, in which her parents emphasized the conservative family values of their Catholic faith. Her parents were so protective, as Gwen would later confess in a 1997 interview with David Keeps of *Details* magazine, that for high-school graduation, instead of attending the typical hotel parties, she had to celebrate at Disneyland and had a midnight curfew. Although her parents were strict and protective, the Stefani household was a loving, supportive place. Peers spent their teenage years rebelling against their parents, but Gwen felt no desire to follow suit. "My parents were very strict," Stefani told *Allure* magazine's Christian Wright in May 2003. "I had to wear white underwear until I finished high school. But they weren't mean strict. They were human, loving, and gave me morals, and I feel I'm very stable because of it."

Gwen was the second of four children (older brother Eric, and younger siblings Jill and Todd) born to high-school sweethearts Dennis and Patti. A former dental assistant, Patti stayed home to raise the kids, while Dennis supported the family with his job as a marketing executive for Yamaha. The company's clientele included many high-profile musicians, who he occasionally allowed Gwen and Eric to meet, including Sting when he was the front man for The Police.

Music figured prominently in the Stefani house. The senior Stefanis were both musically inclined—at one point they were both in a folk group called the Innertubes. Although she shared their admiration for country singer Emmylou Harris, Gwen eschewed their taste for folk and bluegrass music, and Bob Dylan in particular—for Broadway show tunes from such musicals as *The Sound of Music* and *Annie.* Eric liked it all, and exhibited an affinity for making his own music. Eric played the piano and began writing his own songs at an early age. He would often coax Gwen into singing while he played accompaniment. She sang on his earliest attempts at composition, including his first song, "Stick It In The Hole," a song about a pencil sharpener.

Though she would sing for Eric, Gwen describes herself as a shy child. Gwen was involved in dance and sports activities throughout her childhood, in part to address her mother's concerns about her weight. Today the media is as likely to talk about her rock-hard abs as her music, but, as she often reminds reporters, she struggled with her weight growing up. Her mother placed her on her first diet at age twelve. "It was out of my mother's love for me," she told *Details'* writer Keeps. "I don't know if that's so good for a kid to be concerned over that so early. I think it's haunted me in a way."

Nevertheless, Gwen apparently excelled at sports. She even competed for her high-school swim team—during which time she earned the nickname, "Frog."

Academics were a different story. She was a lackluster student. "I was completely satisfied with just being in love with my boyfriend and dreaming about getting married," Stefani recounted to *Blender* magazine's Ariel Levy in December, 2004. "I always thought of myself as really lazy because I was bad at school . . . . Not that I was a bad girl, just that it was hard for me to learn. I couldn't even pay attention. I spent the whole time drawing pictures. The bell would ring and I would be like, 'Gosh the period's over?' I would have just written my boyfriend's name in really sketched out, really nice letters."

A self-described girlie-girl, Gwen developed an early interest in fashion. She learned to sew and later would often make her own outfits. That ability to design and create her own clothes certainly contributed to the development of the singular and eclectic style for which she would later become known.

Gwen admired her brother and credits Eric as being the talented one of the pair. In contrast, Gwen describes herself as passive and lazy. Accomplished in the visual arts in addition to his musical interests, Eric was the creative force pulling his younger sister along for the ride. In a January 2005 interview for the British newspaper, *The Observer,* Gwen told writer Jenny Eliscu, "Everything Eric was into, I got into. He's super creative, and he was this high-school cartoonist and had all these wild artist friends. I don't know if he really was cool or not, but he seemed cool to me."

In his teens, Eric—and consequently Gwen—developed an interest in ska and Two-Tone music. It's not hard to see the attraction, the music was energetic, fun, and raucous with horn sections that blared over a rocking dancehall beat. Ska music emerged in Jamaica in the late 1950s and early 1960s. Ska resulted from the pairing of New Orleans-style rhythm and blues and a mix of Afro-Caribbean musical styles, primarily Mento and Calypso. The Skatalites, a studio band that backed reggae legend Bob Marley, among others, integrated the style into much of the popular music produced in Jamaica at that time.

Though ska would never become a dominant force in mainstream music, it has enjoyed resurgent periods of popularity in England and the United States. "My Boy Lollipop," by London-based Jamaican singer Millie Small, was a major hit that introduced ska to a wider audience in the early 1960s. Desmond Dekker and the Aces were an influential ska group of the same era.

Ska's second iteration emerged in England in the late 1970s and early 1980s. This movement, which blended ska and pop to various degrees, also became known as Two-Tone, in part because many of the bands included both black and white musicians. The Specials, with influential British hits "Gangsters" and "Ghost Town"; Selecter; English Beat, which later split into offshoots General Public and Fine Young Cannibals; and Madness propelled ska back onto the charts.

Thanks in part to heavy airplay on the then-fledgling network MTV, ska made strong inroads in the United States. The English Beat's "Save It For Later" and Madness, with their manic antics on videos such as "Our House" and "House of Fun" influenced late-Eighties American bands including Fishbone and The Untouchables. This generation of West Coast ska musicians were No Doubt's immediate precursors, and were among the bands No Doubt opened for while earning their chops in the Orange County and Los Angeles club circuits.

Madness in particular made a strong impression on Eric. Band mythology pinpoints his purchase of the Madness import single, "Baggy Pants" as a seminal moment in No Doubt's creation. Gwen likens the impact of the first time she heard the record to a bomb being dropped in the Stefani living room. Soon it was all ska and Two-Tone all the time. Along with her passion for the music, Gwen adopted the retro styles common among the genres' fans, known as "rudies." Her enthusiasm was so strong that she even joined Eric and a group

13

of friends for a performance of the Selecter song, "On My Radio" for a high-school talent show.

John Spence, a friend from Loara High School, shared Eric and Gwen's passion for ska. In late December 1986, he and Eric decided to form a band. The pair convinced a somewhat reluctant Gwen to sing harmony to John's lead vocals. Eric played keyboards.

No Doubt, named for John's favorite expression, began by playing at parties and quickly developed an enthusiastic following. Their style fit nicely in the local music scene, which churned with a lively mix of ska, two-tone, funk, and punk.

John took immediately to his role as frontman, pairing his singing/yelling with a high energy, acrobatic stage presence. Gwen took longer to develop her own performance style. After all, what could a pretty girl who often wore dresses on stage do other than sing and stay out of John's trajectory during his back flips? Eric, occupied playing his keyboard, had no such issues to solve.

The trio quickly moved from playing parties to playing "official" gigs. On March 17, 1987, the band played their first club show at Fender's Ballroom in Long Beach: They were the second of fourteen bands on a bill headlined by The Untouchables.

CHAPTER TWO

Get On The Ball

A couple of young musicians from another Anaheim high school had traveled to Long Beach to catch No Doubt's gig at Fender's Ballroom. Saxophone player Eric Carpenter and his bass-playing older brother Dave knew No Doubt's drummer, and brought their friend Tony Kanal along. Tony, a sax-turned-bass player—thanks to Dave's teaching skills—was impressed with their performance. Despite the fact that his musical predilections leaned to hip-hop and funk, he tried out for the band several weeks later.

Then a high-school junior, Tony certainly didn't look the part of a ska band bassist—he wore baggy pants and Mexican sandals to the audition and had long hair—nor did he have experience playing in a band. Despite these potential drawbacks, No Doubt picked him to replace their first bass player, Chris Leal. Tony, who in addition to being a talented musician was extremely organized and determined, soon became the unofficial manager of the band.

All-American-girl Gwen immediately formed a crush on the exotic Tony. His parents, who were Indian, moved to California from England when Tony was eleven years old. Gwen pushed a somewhat unwilling Tony into a romantic relationship soon after he joined the band. Gwen described the scene to *Face* magazine reporter, Jonathan Bernstein in 1997:

"It was 1987 and Tony had just joined the group. We played this party and I knew this was the night I was going to try and kiss him. Me and Tony were walking home and I said, 'Kiss me,' and he wouldn't. And I said, 'But we're in a group together and I want it so bad.' Finally, we kissed down the block. Tony thought that it meant nothing but I was totally in love."

The pair kept their relationship a secret from the other band members for some time. In his role as older brother, Eric was very protective of Gwen. She wasn't well versed in affairs of the heart at that point—before meeting Tony she'd only dated one other guy. Despite their efforts to keep their status a secret, Eric had his suspicions, and made it clear to Tony not to mess with his sister. It would be quite some time, however, before he or anyone else in the band became aware they were a couple.

Throughout 1987—Gwen's senior year of high school—No Doubt played the underground ska/punk scene throughout Orange County and Los Angeles. They rehearsed together each week, twice a week. Everybody in the band had to pitch in to pay for studio time, and with money tight for everyone, they would try to economize where they could.

". . .I remember having to ask my dad for money every time," Gwen later recalled in "The Hub Interview" for the No Doubt Official Web page. "I remember John Spence having a plastic baggie full of pennies and counting them out every week. Remember we used to pay two dollars [to rent] a mic? We'd be like, 'Do we really have to get two mics? We could share.'"

While most of the band was excited about a possible future life in music—they were in the midst of preparing for an upcoming industry gig at L.A.'s Roxy Club—one member was quietly struggling with the present. On December 21, John Spence committed suicide at an Anaheim county park.

His death shocked his friends and band mates. Although unaware of John's true state of mind at the time, Gwen recognized that things weren't always easy for him. "There were some problems there," Gwen recalled during an interview with Jonathan Bernstein for *Spin* magazine in 1997. "He was kind of in and out of high school. His mom kept taking him out of school. He wasn't really in with a bad crowd, but his mom was really paranoid about it. For all the years I knew the guy, I only went to his house one time, but compared to my family—The Brady Bunch family, church every Sunday—it was different."

The band played the gig at the Roxy, believing it would be their last. For several days afterward, while still trying to come to terms with Spence's death, they grappled with the question of whether they should continue. Ultimately they forged ahead in the belief that Spence would have wanted the band to move on.

CHAPTER THREE

Move On

On the heels of Spence's death, No Doubt had one more revelation to handle. Tony and Gwen announced they were dating. Despite Eric's concerns about both Gwen's welfare and the impact a potential split would have on the band, the group got back to the business of playing for fans, honing their skills, and developing their own sound.

In between work and course schedules—Gwen majored in art at Fullerton College—the band would practice at a local rehearsal studio. Guitar player Tom Dumont rehearsed at the same studio with his sister's heavy metal band, Rising, and often looked in on No Doubt's rehearsals. He was frustrated with the local metal scene, so when No Doubt went shopping for a new guitar player in the spring of '88, he auditioned. Proving once again that they were open to diverse musical tastes and fashion choices, No Doubt eagerly brought Tom into the band.

In May, Eric Carpenter (the friend who had brought Tony to No Doubt's first club gig) replaced the band's saxophone player, Alan Meade. After Spence's death, the band had tapped Meade to sing lead vocals. As fate would have it, Meade, aged seventeen, left to marry his pregnant girlfriend and Gwen became the lead singer.

In addition to dealing with typical hassles of being the only girl in the band (the burping, the farting, the jokes about burping and farting, among other guy classics), Stefani had to contend with an under-lying chauvinism typical at that time. "When I first started singing, there weren't very many female singers in the scene," Stefani told *BAM* magazine's Wendy Hermanson in November, 1995.

"Whenever we went to a club, I would always be looked upon as a tagalong girlfriend—'Where's your wristband?!' But as soon as I finished a show, the same people would be, like, 'Oooh. I can't believe you were up there!' And the attitudes of the girls in the beginning! More like, 'Bitch! Who does she think she is?!'"

Those attitudes began to change as the band drew greater exposure and became staples on the underground ska/punk scene. They opened for Fishbone and The Untouchables (albeit no longer at the bottom of the bill) and for the Red Hot Chili Peppers. In addition to picking up fans, No Doubt was also getting to know other musicians who were a part of the scene. Red Hot Chili Peppers' bassist Flea (a.k.a. Michael Balzary) produced two demos for the fledgling band.

In the summer of 1989, Adrian Young joined the band. Young was a big fan of No Doubt's music. He was so determined to grab the drummer's chair that he lied about his experience: He claimed he'd been drumming since 1983, when he'd only been at it for about a year. In addition to being a big ska and punk fan, he'd grown up listening to the likes of Led Zeppelin, Jimmy Hendrix, and Bob Marley.

As the band added new members with different musical backgrounds, No Doubt drifted from its ska roots. Dumont reflected on his unwitting role in that evolution in a piece he later wrote for *Guitar* magazine in 1997:

"I didn't really have a deep knowledge of the ska scene. I tried to fit in quickly, but I never seriously studied the ska idiom. I never, for example, sat down with a Madness record and tried to learn the guitar riffs. I kind of picked up the general gist of things from the other guys in the band. It turned out to be a blessing in disguise, because we ended up sounding unlike any other ska band."

And as they gained more confidence in their songwriting abilities, the band acknowledged the shift and began to purposely develop their own sound out of those divergent experiences. Reaction to the move was mixed, as original fans and hardcore ska and Two Tone devotees would later accuse the band of selling out. For the band, it was an exciting direction. . .one that Kanal saw as inevitable.

". . .Eric. . .was big on soundtracks like *The Sound Of Music*," Tony explained in an interview with Mike Gee for the Web zine *This Swirling Sphere* in 1997. "Adrian (Young, drums) grew up on '70s rock like Hendrix, Journey, Steely Dan; Tom (Dumont, guitar) was a big Kiss fan who then got into Black Sabbath, Judas Priest, and all those heavy metal and Brit rock outfits, and for me, Prince was the first major musical thing, so I guess when you take all that, we're bound to produce an open-ended sound. None of us would want it any other way. You know, just one sound would be so limiting and boring."

Gwen commented on their development in Wendy Hermanson's article for *BAM* after *Tragic Kingdom* was released: "I look at our band as kinda like The Police," Stefani mused. "They had the reggae/ska thing happening, but they're a rock band. Our roots are ska, but ska just bubbles under in our music. We don't label our sound by that term."

By their third album, Dumont acknowledged in *Guitar World* that he saw a full-fledged rock band: "We started adding much more rock-sounding guitars, to the point where I think *Tragic Kingdom* is a fairly rock guitar album. There are a lot of distorted parts, and really not a straight ska song on the whole record. I think the band has evolved quite a bit, and, in a way, my style has come full circle."

Regardless of the changes, they continued to expand their fan base. That summer, the band played their first out-of-state show in Arizona. Though they didn't pull in the large crowds they'd come to expect on their home turf—there were 100 people in the crowd that first night—it was a start in the right direction.

CHAPTER FOUR

Trapped In A Box

I n 1990, thanks to gigs opening for shows with headliners such as the Red Hot Chili Peppers and Ziggy Marley, No Doubt was beginning to capture the ear of the college crowd. Despite their growing fan base and attention from college radio stations, the press ignored them and labels wouldn't talk to them. Their unique sound defied definition, and it worked against them. After the success of *Tragic Kingdom*, Tony shared the irony of their early history with Mike Gee for the Web zine, *This Swirling Sphere:*

"While record companies were running around signing up everybody that could play a note in Orange County, we were totally overlooked. Even the press overlooked us. It got frustrating. We'd be sitting there reading these articles about the Orange County scene and there'd be all these bands and no No Doubt. . .

"And it was a problem with the record companies because they didn't know how to pigeon-hole us. But we seem to have overcome that now. They call the sound 'No Doubt'. We have stories of other record companies going out and trying to find bands like No Doubt now. It's so funny.

"For so many years you have these record companies telling you 'you've gotta focus, you've gotta focus,' you've gotta have all the songs sounding the same and then you overcome that and people are running round telling you how good it is that you have such a broad range of sounds and that the songs are so different. And we've always been that."

Finally, No Doubt captured the attention of someone who "got" their music. Tony Ferguson, an A&R

man with L.A.-based label Interscope followed the band's progress closely. "At the time, Pearl Jam and Nirvana were breaking, and nobody wanted to hear an eight-piece horn section with a blonde girl from Orange County doing ska-retro-disco-metal-funk," Ferguson told *Taxi.com* interviewer Michael Laskow. "But the kids did. I would go to the shows in Orange County and up here, and they were selling out. The Whisky, The Troubadour—they were selling places out."

He convinced Interscope head Jimmy Iovine to catch one of their shows and in August of '91, No Doubt signed a contract with the label. The band made their eponymous debut LP for a meager $13,000. Between October and January of 1992, the band commuted between Orange County and Los Angeles to lay down tracks. Recording sessions were sandwiched in between the demands of work and classes— at the time, Tom was a music major, Gwen was an art major, Tony and Adrian were both studying psychology, and Eric Carpenter was pursuing journalism.

The excitement of having obtained label backing began to wear off soon after they signed the contract. In a 1995 interview with *BAM's* Wendy Hermanson, Dumont and Stefani described their disappointment with Interscope's contribution to their debut.

"At the time, we were finishing up an indie CD that we were going to put out ourselves," said Dumont. "[Interscope] decided they wanted to sign us, and they were going to give us some money. So, we thought, 'OK, let's redo the CD in a really good studio.'"

"And we thought we were recording in a really good studio," Stefani added. "But looking back, we were naive. It was almost like an independent release, anyway—there was no push for the record [by Interscope] and no kind of support at all. Everything we did on that record, we did ourselves. We did get tour support, though, so we toured the U.S. once."

Of their fourteen songs, "Trapped in a Box" seemed the most likely single. A short sketch of a poem by Tom about how he hated getting sucked into watching television provided the basis for the song. "It was so weird back then because there was nobody that was really a lyricist, that took on the role," Gwen recalled in "The Hub Interview." "I mean, Eric would write lyrics, but we would all contribute. For "Trapped in a Box," that was one song where each person. . .we all sat down at the coffee table and okay, 'everybody try to write a verse.' It was like an exercise because we were all so inexperienced. We were still learning. It was such an accomplishment when it all came together. We were really very proud of it because it had a message behind it."

Its development from poem to finished product is still typical of the way No Doubt create their songs. One member may come up with an initial idea—whether it was a concept, lyrics, a guitar lick, or a bass line—and the group would collaborate to various degrees on all aspects of it. They sometimes work together or an individual would go off on their own to work on a discreet element until they had a finished song. The final product may or may not bear resemblance to the original kernel.

"It's amazing how. . .it becomes a song" Gwen said in the same interview. "I can't really hear all of it in my head. It's pretty neat how it all comes together as a group, how it evolves. It takes a long time to evolve into a song."

With Gwen's singular vocals, coupled with clever lyrics— *Trapped in a box of tremendous size/It distorts my vision, it closes my eyes/Attracts filthy flies and pollutes in the skies/Suck up our lives and proliferates lies/Trapped in a box*—overlaid by a heavily ska-inflected beat, No Doubt was convinced they had the makings of a hit.

The album, which the band dedicated to Spence, was released in March of 1992. Interscope shopped "Trapped" to radio stations, but unfortunately for the band, Pearl Jam and Nirvana, along with a host of other grunge bands had just taken over the air waves. Commercial radio was loath to take a chance on No Doubt's upbeat ska-pop confection. Play on L.A.'s major-market KROQ would have influenced radio stations nationwide to follow suit, but even their hometown station refused to give them airtime. As Adrian recalls, KROQ's then-program director remarked, "It would take an act of God for this band to get on the radio." Lacking even the support of local radio, the album sold a meager 30,000 copies.

As a result of the cool reception to "Trapped" by radio stations, Interscope paid for the band to tour, but little else. Soon after its release, the band embarked on multiple multi-state tours in support of their first album. The two Western states and one national headlining tours were a far cry from rock 'n' roll luxury. The five members of the band, their three-man horn section, a roadie, their manager/soundman, and all of their equipment were crammed into two vans.

No Doubt's promo budget allotment was "conservative" at best. Fueled by Kanal's organizational skills and seemingly innate business sense, the band did much of the legwork by themselves. Even though the label was unwilling to lavish huge sums on No Doubt, Interscope's Ferguson was impressed with their focus and determination.

"They are the smartest people I know," he told Michael Laskow in an interview for *Taxi.com*. "They took care of themselves. They put their own merchandising together. They got their Web site together. They got their fan base together. I mean they were very, very motivated in keeping the fan base together. It was growing all the time."

Apparently Interscope's mailroom staff was none too thrilled when the band would drop off flyers. "The mailroom guys would cringe because it would take them all day to mail them out," Ferguson recalls. "There were literally hundreds and hundreds and hundreds of these mail-outs, and their fan base was getting bigger."

The label did give No Doubt money to make a video for "Trapped in a Box," which they filmed after the first leg of their Western States tour. Despite—or perhaps because of—the limits of their $5,000 budget, the band made a video that is not only amusing, but also projects No Doubt's frenetic but fun personality. "Trapped," alternates between concept and performance. In the opening scene, a fat, balding man sits passively, watching a TV screen with a beer in one hand and a remote control in the other while people zip through the room. The next shot is of the band performing and jumping around in a tiny

room, wearing outfits they typically wore on stage, and generally being offbeat and silly. This shot captures the energy of their live shows. The third scene is the band performing again, this time in a larger, more formal setting. The boys are dolled up in suits, bow ties, and suspenders (except for Adrian, who sports boxers and nothing else), and Gwen gets the glam treatment as a Forties-era chanteuse.

Its energy and humor evoked the verve of videos from MTV's salad days. Despite its ethos of Madness' "Our House," MTV ignored the video. No Doubt got back on the road for the rest of the summer and much of the fall. In addition to headlining their own small club gigs, they opened shows for Public Enemy, Pato Banton, and Special Beat.

CHAPTER FIVE

Let's Get Back

Buoyed by their reception at shows across the country, No Doubt started working on material for what would become the *Tragic Kingdom* album in March of 1993. Through the rest of that year and part of the next, they brought songs to Interscope. The label continually sent them back to the drawing board.

Despite their record contract and the release of their first album, No Doubt was not in an enviable position. The next two years sorely tested the band's mettle and they lost a few members along the way.

When Eric Carpenter quit the band in the spring of 1994 to finish up his journalism degree at Cal State Fullerton, things weren't looking good for the band's future. Interscope still wasn't ready to let No Doubt move forward on a new album. It was a sporadic process: It eventually took two and a half years and recording sessions in eleven studios before the label released *Tragic Kingdom*.

Interscope's continual pressure on the band to adjust their sound exacerbated the delays. The label paired them with Matthew Wilder, producer of the '80s pop hit "Break My Stride," a decision that later paid off, but along with other "suggestions," initially rankled the band.

"This is a very weird thing to talk about," Tony told Chris Heath in a 1997 *Rolling Stone* interview. "because I don't want it to come across that we changed our songs and we were just beat down like baby seals. One of the reasons this record took so long to come out is that we withstood a lot of pressures and we were unwilling to compromise on a lot of things. *Tragic Kingdom* is a battleground. It was the outcome of three years of struggle."

Band members, in addition to writing, rehearsing, producing demo tracks, and performing, were still working to make ends meet. In a personal essay published in the *Orange Country Register* in January 1997, Carpenter wrote about his decision to leave the band: "The band didn't pay full-time wages but required full-time commitment. I was one of several members throughout the band's history who needed to find other avenues when times got tough. In my case, it was time to return to journalism school."

Derided as the "Pete Best of No Doubt," he reminded his detractors that success was not a foregone conclusion.

"We played where we could, toured in rented vans, lived on measly per diems, and considered ourselves fortunate for a bed at Motel 6."

By the start of '93, No Doubt was ready to record a second album, given the working title of "Tragic Kingdom"—named after Eric Stefani's tune about Walt Disney's beneficent dream taking a twisted turn in careless hands. Carpenter described that period as immensely frustrating, with repeated delays from the record company. After much soul searching, Carpenter quit the band in the Spring of 1994.

Eric Stefani was beginning to have doubts of his own around the same time. Eric was the creative heart and soul of the group. Although songwriting was collaborative, Eric pushed their development to a higher level. In "The Hub Interview" in 1997, Gwen described the intensity and drive Eric brought to the songwriting process. "Our teacher, I think, in some way[s] was my brother, who was really aware of detailing. And there would be times where. . .we would spend days going over one transition—one tiny little beat section. Nobody would even realize how much time we put into it. And it was really complex. And then the next day we would come, and Eric had been up all night long rewriting that same part, and had a whole new bridge. And all the work we put into it the day before was almost wasted. I think all of that studying and having to go through all that was a way of us learning how to do it. And now Tony and Adrian are really good at that. I think it comes from having to go through the torture of the Eric Stefani school and this really obscene detailing and taking a lot of time and then changing it and changing it and changing it."

As the band played tug of war—practically song by song—with Interscope over the integrity of the band's sound, Eric became frustrated and started to disengage from the band. It was a gradual process—he was involved through the making of *Tragic Kingdom* and would continue to collaborate with the band over the years. He left that year to pursue his work as an animator on *The Simpsons* fulltime.

"I was trying too hard to put my personality, or my being, on this planet through the music," Eric told Chris Heath for a 1997 profile of No Doubt in *Rolling Stone*. "And I didn't know how to express myself any other way. So when that was compromised, I was lost. But I think I found myself more by losing that and having to act as a human."

Eric's departure was tough on the band. No longer able to rely on Eric for ideas, the remaining members of the group took greater control over the music. It was particularly difficult for Gwen, who had

always leaned on Eric's leadership for direction. While she felt comfortable onstage, she had yet to develop confidence in her abilities as a lyricist. She questioned whether she had anything significant to say.

She soon found her subject matter close to home. Tony and Gwen had dated since they met in 1987. In the early '90s, they began having problems, thanks, surely, to the sheer amount of time they spent together because of the band. In addition to dating and spending time together for the band, they also worked together at the same department store. "I think he started feeling really claustrophobic," Gwen later told *Rolling Stone's* Chris Heath. "And he'd never had any kind of experience, as far as seeing other girls, since he was sixteen years old. Of course, he was going out with the raddest girl in the world."

They broke up in 1994, amidst the troubles with Interscope and Eric's departure. Both cared about each other and neither one wanted to leave the band. It wasn't easy on either one of them, and it took years to deal with, but they managed to tough it out. And according to Tom Dumont, they worked hard to keep their rift from affecting the rest of the band. "It's interesting every day," Dumont told *Liner Notes* magazine in January 1997. "Sometimes I tell Tony, 'you should have just stayed with her. It would be a lot easier. Everybody would be happy, getting along.' But people have to follow their own hearts. I think they still care deeply for each other but it's hard to breakup with your girlfriend and then live with her. That's a tall order. They've done a great job of pulling it off. When we're all together, we get along pretty good."

Tony, or rather, their relationship, the breakup, and the issues they faced post break up, became Gwen's muse. Her efforts to hash out her feelings in her lyrics resulted in multiple tracks for the album: "Hey You," "End It On This," "Don't Speak," "Sunday Morning," "Spiderwebs," and "Happy Now?" all deal with the subject in one way or another. As painful as it must have been to get through, their break up was fortuitous. "Don't Speak," "Spiderwebs," and "Sunday Morning," were released as singles, and they would later help to propel *Tragic Kingdom's* stratospheric sales.

Tony was very supportive of her choices—even though those songs often prompted the public to vilify or at least shake their heads at his lack of judgment in spurning Gwen. "It's very tough," he admitted to *Spin* magazine's Jonathan Bernstein in 1996. "I care about her a lot. I'm not given the opportunity— nor do I want it— to write my own lyrics. But hopefully people with some logic will realize that it wasn't just me, that it's not just a one-sided thing. I'm not such a bad guy."

Gwen, for her part, consistently backed Tony in the press and good-naturedly joked about her overbearing personality in that regard. "I forced Tony to go out with me," she told Bernstein in the same interview. "He wasn't even interested. When we made out that first night, I think he thought it was more of a one-night kiss. But then we started going out and after the first year, I was going 'When are we getting married?'"

At the very least, Tony and Gwen had the distraction of solving how to get Interscope to back an album release of their new material. Stymied by the label's lack of support, they took matters into their own hands. No Doubt built a makeshift studio in the garage of the Beacon Street house where several members of the band lived (at this point Gwen still lived at home). The tracks "Total Hate" and "Snakes" were among the ten *Tragic Kingdom* B-Sides they recorded. None of the current members were involved in the creation of "Total Hate '95." It was an early work, penned in part by John Spence. "Snakes" eventually wound up on the *Beavis and Butthead Do America* movie soundtrack.

Early in 1995, they released the Beacon Street Collection CD on their own and sold it at shows and local record stores—it was essentially a bootleg recording of their own music. They quickly sold out of the first thousand copies they'd produced. Interscope decided it was time to get the next album rolling.

CHAPTER SIX

Tragic Kingdom

No Doubt's gamble paid off, but it was helped along by a little bit of luck. After the tracks on *Tragic Kingdom* had been recorded and edited, Interscope's Tony Ferguson brought the roughs to Paul Palmer to get his opinion. Palmer was a co-owner of the boutique label Trauma Records, which recently had become an Interscope partner. Trauma had just broken the British grunge band, Bush.

"I thought they were fantastic the minute I heard the music," Palmer later told *Spin's* Jonathan Bernstein. "It was all there, even in its roughest stages "I had a feeling about the band I couldn't let go of." Palmer's team took over from that point on, and the band benefited not only from a label that "got" their music, but one whose small stature translated into a more focused effort to promote their welfare.

Interscope still had a financial stake in the band's success, and despite Palmer's enthusiasm, Tony Ferguson recalls that the label's executives were still biting their fingernails over the band's commercial viability.

"There were always questions about what we were going to do with this band, because rock was still in this alternative grunge thing," Ferguson told *Taxi.com's* Michael Laskow. "Here we had this ska-influenced, pop-ish hook-driven band with a blonde girl singer. You've got Alanis Morissette, who is the epitome of the angry woman, and here we had Gwen Stefani, who is a little bit more of the antithesis of that and is just enjoying herself." Stefani's quirky fashion choices likely caused Interscope some consternation as well. How do you explain a skater chick in Doc Martins sporting a glam '40s-era hair do and a bindi on her forehead? (A bindi, by the way, is the "holy dot" traditionally worn by Hindu women, which was believed to have protective powers. Today, it serves merely as decoration, and though typically just a red dot made with vermillion, it comes in many colors, shapes, materials, and designs. Gwen loved the bindis worn by Tony's mother and her friends, and adopted a jewel bindi as part of her own eclectic style.)

"But music is the same merry-go-round," Ferguson continued "Trends go round and round and round, but every time they come back around—whether it's metal, or rock, or pop, or disco, or dance music, or whatever—there is always a new twist."

The irony is that Gwen had similar questions about where she fit into to female rock universe. "Yeah, I never felt really strong growing up," she told *Rolling Stone's* Neil Strauss in January 2002. "I didn't know where I fit in. All the women around me that I could look at were in bands like L7 or Hole. They were angry, and I didn't really feel like that. And the other ones were these folky girls, so there wasn't really anybody, until I discovered Blondie. She was sexy and she wasn't ashamed to be rocking out, and to me, that's having it all."

The label was already committed to the release at this point, and they—and Gwen—would have to trust the public to figure it out for themselves. In anticipation of the album's release, No Doubt went on the road with the Warped Tour, a stadium road show sponsored by sneaker company Vans that combined performances by alternative bands and exhibitions of extreme sports like BMX and skateboarding, from August through September of 1995. *Tragic Kingdom* was released in October.

At first nobody seemed to notice the album, but later that fall, KROQ began playing the single, "Just A Girl." In December, No Doubt performed at KROQ's annual holiday concert, where they first met label mates, Bush. No Doubt was slated to open for Bush on their upcoming tour. Their initial meeting was less than auspicious, as they later confessed to Neil Strauss of *Rolling Stone.*

As the story goes, Dumont was a huge fan of Nigel Pulsford, Bush's guitarist. Unfortunately, Dumont was very drunk by the time he arrived at the KROQ show. His first move upon barging into Bush's dressing room was to insult Pulsford's choice of guitars (Pulsford used Fenders), and proceeded to get himself kicked out. The next day, Bush's record company threatened to pull No Doubt off the schedule if they couldn't manage to control themselves.

Bush lead singer Gavin Rossdale's first impression of Stefani, on the other hand, boded well for inter-band relations. "The first thing he said to me was, "You're gorgeous,'" she told Johnathan Bernstein in a 1997 *YM* article. "I wasn't looking to go out with a boy in a band—especially one who's that good-looking. I'm usually attracted to guys with personalities, ones that make me laugh. That's what I think is sexy—not some dude with flowing curls who's tall and gorgeous."

Rossdale won her over quickly, however, and within days they started a romantic relationship that would eventually result in their marriage in 2002. It was a significant moment for Stefani, who was finally able to move on after her break up with Kanal.

"I couldn't believe he liked me!" Gwen told Bernstein. "I'd been down about the Tony thing for so long that my self-esteem was way down, too. And suddenly this guy thinks I'm great—and he has a British accent!"

Thanks to early support from KROQ, "Just A Girl" quickly gained momentum. By January, MTV was running the video all the time. The clip shows the boys hanging out together in a drab, rundown room. Separated from the band and placed in a dainty, finely appointed dressing room, a bindi-adorned, midriff baring Gwen rocks out by herself. Apparently the music-buying public had no qualms about the track's decidedly new wave bent. That same month, the album debuted on *Billboard's* Top 200 at #175 and "Just A Girl" reached #10.

With lyrics such as *'Cause I'm just a girl, little ol' me / Don't let me out of your sight / I'm just a girl, all pretty and petite / so don't let me have any rights,* "Just A Girl" became an instant modern feminist pop classic. The song hit a nerve with female listeners, who could relate to Stefani's sarcastic commentary on the universal constraints—major and minor, external and internal—that confine women.

"I never dreamed that it would become anything that it became," she told Jonathan Bernstein in a 1997 interview for *The Face* magazine. "I was never a feminist but the more time went by, I realized that I was in a male-dominated society and things would affect me. I was never outraged by it, but the main thing was I would get really scared about things. I thought, it really sucks that I have to be frightened every time I leave the house. That's what triggered the song for me, just having these fears and experiences. A lot of things happen to you when you're a girl, like you're walking down the street and a guy whistles at you and you're like, what? What are you thinking? Am I just on display like a toy or a piece of candy? Next day you walk down the street and no one whistles at you and you think, I must look really ugly. Like I said, I never meant it to be any kind of feminist statement, but little girls really get into it, they go, 'You kicked ass!'"

The inspiration for the song came from her father's constant concern for her safety growing up.

"I got the idea when my dad used to yell at me for going to Tony's house and coming home real late," Gwen told *Circus* magazine's Jessica Letkemann in February 1997. "I don't think a lot of guys know what a burden it is to be a girl sometimes." The sentiments are universal, but the song could also be read as a personal manifesto for Stefani. She's grown up in a protective bubble created by her parents, her brother Eric, and her relationship with Kanal.

I'm just a girl, living in captivity / Your rule of thumb / Make me worry some / I'm just a girl, what's my destiny? What I've succumbed to / Is making me numb.

It was a nurturing, comfortable place, but she's realized that it's a constraining one as well. When she sings *I've had it up to here! / Am I making myself clear*—she declares that it's a world she'll no longer accept.

Live, the song becomes even more rebellious, as Stefani gets the audience into the act. In a 1996 concert review in *Rolling Stone* described what had already become a nightly ritual performance of the anthemic song: "After goading a 'boys only' singalong (complete with middle finger salute), she got the 'dear, sweet, little girls' to scream 'F*** you, I'm a Girl'. This must have gone over great with the parents in attendance."

Apparently her own mother was none too pleased with Stefani's rendition of the song at a promotional gig at a local Virgin Megastore in late 1995. Mrs. Stefani had invited relatives to the show and had asked her daughter to refrain from swearing during the performance. Gwen, irritated by her mother's request, was unable to contain herself.

Her mother wouldn't speak to her for a week afterward, despite the fact that Gwen was heading out on tour. Though defiant in the moment, Gwen admits that she was terribly upset that her mother was angry with her.

Her young female fans didn't seem to mind. Most guys in the audience got caught up with the raucous spirit of the song as well, but some missed the boat entirely. In a 1997 interview with David A. Keeps for *Details*, she shared her frustration over the behavior of some of her male fans at one concert. The audience was chanting during her performance of "Just A Girl." "I'm like, 'Cool, they're really getting into it.' And then all of a sudden it's, 'Show me your tits!' I'm up there making a point about how I feel being a chick. Even though maybe the song is not as cool as a Courtney Love song, it is my life and how I've been meant to feel throughout ten years of being in a man's business, and suddenly they just totally miss the whole point and I just feel like a whore. Like, what am I doing up there in front of all these boys with a little top on? Maybe I'm asking for it, you know?"

If the rest of American males had yet to crawl out of the stone age, at least her bandmates were on board. Dumont wrote the song's driving riffs, and the reception it got was a point of pride. "It feels great," Dumont told Bob Gulla in an interview for *Guitar* magazine.

"I co-wrote "Just A Girl," and when it started getting played it was really thrilling, and it gave me confidence. I had finally put together something that worked and that people could react to." It was a feeling that Dumont and the rest of the band would get to enjoy for some time to come.

CHAPTER SEVEN

Happy Now?

The band was on a roll by this point. In January, they appeared on *Late Night* with Conan O'Brien, and by March they were performing "Just A Girl" on *The Late Show* for David Letterman. Later that spring, the band went on tour as the opening act for Bush.

The sixty-date tour was a good gig for No Doubt. Bush's album had already hit multi-Platinum status, and No Doubt's opening sets won over many a die-hard grunge fan. The tour provided great exposure for the band, but Stefani's compatriots were less than thrilled about her budding relationship with Bush frontman Rossdale.

"Everybody was against it," Stefani recalled in an interview with Ariel Levy for *Blender* in 2004. "It was a very crazy time. There was already my breakup with Tony, and we were enjoying success for the first time and having outside things come in to our little band, our little family. And then I met Gavin. It was really lonely, because I felt like nobody wanted me to go out with him. My ex-boyfriend and all of my, like, brothers in the band were saying, 'You are not gonna go out with that guy!'"

In addition to concerns that the relationship would interfere with No Doubt's efforts to capitalize on their new-found momentum, the guys were leary of Rossdale's intentions. He was a musician, after all, and Stefani, despite her commanding onstage presence and budding role as rock-star goddess, led a very sheltered life. She'd never been out with anyone but Kanal before she met Rossdale.

If their relationship was having an effect, it wasn't evident in Stefani's high-powered live performances.

She'd come a long way from her early days in the band, when she was completely unsure of how to behave in front of an audience. Perhaps taking cues from John Spence's example, she was bold and athletic—dancing, karate kicking, pogoing, running, and prowling all over the stage—and if that didn't suffice to get the crowd going, she'd climb the speakers. She'd often throw in a few push ups for good measure. These were not dainty performances—by the end of a night, she'd be soaked in sweat from her efforts. The only thing that managed to slow her down was the foot she broke during a show in May of that year.

The next single to come out was the song "Spiderwebs," which Stefani and Kanal co-wrote. The song is something everyone can relate to: Dodging an oblivious admirer who won't stop calling. *You take advantage of what's mine / You're taking up my time / Don't have the courage inside me / to tell you please just let me be.* The character in the song's only recourse is to screen calls: *Sorry I'm not home right now / I'm walking into spiderwebs / So leave a message / And I'll call you back / A likely story, but leave a message.* The video switches between scenes of the band performing in a baroque hall to a rather staid crowd to images of the band being enveloped in marauding telephone wires.

In June, their second single reached hit *Billboard's* Number 5 position and the band embarked on their first international tour. On the first leg, they wowed European crowds. Later that summer their focus shifted to Asia, with dates in Australia, New Zealand, Indonesia, and Japan. In July, *Tragic Kingdom* went Platinum, and a month later, the album was certified Double-Platinum. When they returned, they kicked off the MTV Music Video Awards, playing their set on top of the Radio City Music Hall Marquee.

Despite the fact that Stefani was still living at home (when the band wasn't on the road), No Doubt was officially living the rock 'n' roll dream. The media coverage—radio, TV, and print—was phenomenal. The only problem was that the lion's share of the attention was focused on Stefani. The media couldn't contain their fascination with this platinum blonde singer, and the questions were endless. *How will she do her hair? How does she get those washboard abs and how much of them will she show? Why does she wear a bindi on your forehead? Is this song about her break up with Tony? Why did he break up with Gwen? Is she dating Gavin Rossdale?* Her very unique fashion sense, and the fact that she inspired so many female fans—dubbed Gwenabees—to copy her look, all attracted intense coverage. *US* magazine's Kim France explained the media's obsession with No Doubt's singer in a 1997 article: "Part of it is that she's just so cute. Then there's her vampish, playful performance style: One moment she's stalking across the stage like a rapper; the next, she's furiously pogoing. But most compelling is her truly unique sense of style. With the platinum '40s hairdo, the Indian jewel between her eyes, the constantly bare midriff, and the Southern California skateboard gear, Stefani is part Barbie doll, part club kid, part Hindu goddess."

Even in the music press, the rest of the band was getting short shrift. In their first feature in the November 1996 issue of music magazine *Spin,* Stefani was on the cover, alone. The rest of the band had a hard time dealing with the discrepancy—they'd now posed for too many band photos where it was obvious that the photographer was zeroing in solely on Gwen. Publicly, the boys were diplomatic about the situation, but wanted to make it clear that No Doubt was not Stefani's solo act.

"Before this record came out, we were always a band, a democracy—this was never an issue," Kanal told David A. Keeps for the April 1997 issue of *Details*. "There's a natural tendency for the media to gravitate toward lead singers—particularly females—and if you've seen Gwen perform, you can see that she deserves it. It's not something we've been dealing with for a long time, but I think we've gotten used to it."

In the same article, which, incidentally, was about Gwen, as part of *Details'* special issue: "Violent Femmes: Eight Sisters With Voices and Looks to Die For," Gwen was vociferous in her emphasis that it was an equal partnership.

"It's not like Gwen Stefani and the No Doubt background loser boys," she told Keeps. "I would feel naked without them."

Stefani, tried to keep the situation in perspective. "Everybody just wants to focus on the girl," Stefani told Mike Boehm of the *Los Angeles Times* in February, 1997. "I think that's the one outside stress thing that has come into the band. We're getting over it. The others sit and bag on me constantly now. Like, 'On MTV News, Gwen broke her foot last night blah blah blah. . .and in less important news, Tom Dumont was found dead.'"

The band worked through some of their issues by

addressing the problem in the video for their third single, "Don't Speak." The lyrics were inspired by Stefani's feelings about the break up with Kanal. They worked off the tone of the song, which was infused with the regret and pain of lyrics like *Don't speak / I know what your thinking / I don't need your reasons / Don't tell me 'cause it hurts* to play a band on the verge of breaking up.

The story line of the video focuses on Gwen being singled out for a photo shoot and on the band's reaction, both at the photo shoot and during a subsequent rehearsal.

Tensions and tempers were running high, and the band actually was on the brink of disbanding. They were actually fighting during the filming of the video. "We were on tour for too long and we weren't getting along," Stefani told *Details*. "We thought the saddest thing we could do was a video about the band breaking up, 'cause we really thought we might."

Although the video couldn't change the fact that Gwen commanded more media attention, it proved to be a cathartic project for the band. "I'm very proud of that video," Kanal told Jonathan Bernstein in a May 1997 article for *The Face Magazine*. "I think it made everyone in the band really realize how everyone felt and I think, for us three, for us to know that Gwen realizes what's going on is very important because sometimes it's easy to think that she doesn't. I think the video made it pretty clear that she knew what was going on. Her guilty look when she looks at us and she's doing the photo by herself is brilliant. That look tells a million words."

The band addressed the same issue once more in the video for their fourth single off the album, "Excuse Me Mr." This time they took a humorous approach, with Gwen jumping into view of the camera lens every time it was trained on another member of the band. These shots were interspersed with black and white scenes of Gwen playing a damsel in distress, tied to railroad tracks by the rest of her band.

"Excuse Me Mr." was another track with a driving, frenetic beat. The lyrics suggest a character coming to the realization that her relationship is over and her former love interest (could it be Kanal?) is no longer there to act as her knight in shining armor.

It's almost as if I'm tied to the tracks / And I'm waiting for him / to rescue me / The funny thing is / He's not going to come / He's not going to find me / This is a matter of fact / The desire you lack / This is the way I guess it has to be. . .

As frustrated as the rest of the band was about Stefani's sudden transformation into a star, life in the limelight was not always as pleasant as it would seem. Having exposed her feelings about her relationship with Kanal in *Tragic Kingdom,* reporters would sometimes step over the line. Both Jonathan Bernstein and Kennedy, in interviews for *Face* magazine and *Spin,* respectively, asked whether the singer had lost her virginity to Kanal. It was a difficult line of questioning for Stefani, who had been brought up in a strict Catholic family.

In response to Bernstein's line of questioning, Stefani replied, "I would never tell you that! Are you crazy? I would never tell anyone that. I have pretty strong feelings about that. If any girls were to ask me what my advice would be, completely wait as long as possible, wait till you're married. I think it's really a sacred thing. It's different when you get older and you have a boyfriend. . .It's such a blessing that God gave us, we should be able to respect it. I'm not going to talk about that stuff any more."

Stefani had already come up against the frustration of the music industry shying away from the band because they didn't fit into an easy category to sell. But she found out early on that the political world could be just as rigid in its acceptance of differences—even subtle ones—of opinion.

"We were playing a Rock for Choice benefit," she told Wendy Hermanson for a November 1995 article in *BAM.* "They were all excited about us and everything, 'cause I'm a girl. Whatever. Anyway, my own feelings on abortion are pro-choice, but I personally don't feel right about it. I'm glad that no one can make that choice for me, though. So I said to the audience, 'You know, if it were me, I would not choose to have an abortion, but I'm glad I have the choice.' After the show, everyone was so pissed off at me for saying that. . .Hey, it was a pro-choice benefit. . .there was nothing wrong with what I said."

Despite the fact that she epitomized and wholeheartedly embraced feminist ideals, she often came under fire for admitting her vulnerabilities and for just enjoying being feminine. Her detractors pointed to her midriff baring shirts—despite the fact that they were paired with utilitarian pants and Doc Martins—and sex appeal as proof that she was neither a valid female role model nor rocker.

The notion that she could be considered sexy came as a surprise to Stefani, and it took her some time to get used to it. "I've never thought of myself as sexual, in that I tried to get up on stage and be sexy," she told Mike Boehm of the *Los Angeles Times* in February 1997. "If people think I might be, that's fine. I decided that if I just reflect the things that make me happy and move me, that's worked best for me, and other people can relate to it."

"I just recently got ragged on for the girly stuff," she told Bernstein. "Maybe I should be more of a tough chick. But I'm not. That's not me. I love makeup. I love getting my hair done. I love getting pedicures. I'm the furthest thing from a rock chick."

Stefani may not look or act like a stereotypical tough rock chick, but if you scratch just under the surface, you'll find a woman of steel. The Orange County underground punk/ska scene of the late '80s to early '90s was a male-dominated world. Stefani was one of the few women musicians in the scene—onstage or in the audience. The mosh pits were a tough place even for guys—and most women were content watch live shows from the back of the room. But at No Doubt shows, Stefani's antics on stage inspired women in the audience to get into the center of things.

"It's gradually changed into this whole bonding thing between all the girls at the shows," Stefani told

Wendy Hermanson of *BAM* in November of 1995. They have their songs—they consider them their songs—that they can [mosh] to."

"Gwen's pretty amazing," Kanal told Mike Gee in May 1996 for music Web site, *This Swirling Sphere,* ". . .Something happens that really transcends the music. Gwen gets the girls into it, lets them participate whereas with a lot of other bands it's just a testosterone thing. Our audience is spread right across the board. Gwen will definitely get the girls involved, give them songs that are their songs and their time to get boosted, be in the pit whatever. Everybody feels part of it; nobody gets left out."

And really, the energy from the fans was what it was all about. The degree of the response surprised Stefani. "For me, I know myself," she confessed, amused, to Vinnie Penn in the February 1997 issue of *Circus* magazine. "I know what a dork I am and where I come from. I would never look at myself and think that I could have any kinda influence on anyone. I'm just me."

Even as the fans dubbed Gwenabees slavishly copied her evolving styles, Stefani took it in stride—often joking that they looked far better than she did. Critics pointed to her fashion following as yet more proof that she was just another pretty face, rather than a "real" musician. If it bothered her, she didn't let on, and focused instead on the positive aspects of that adulation. "It's amazing to have a connection with girls all over the world that you've never met," she told Lou Carlozo in a *Chicago Tribune* article in January, 1997. "No matter where you are in the world, we've shared a lot of the same experiences, have a lot of the same interests. It's great for me to be able to relate."

It did bother Stefani, however, when people got the facts wrong about the band. "I like people to know that we're a homegrown band," Stefani said in an interview with *Teen Vogue* for the Spring 2002 issue. "I don't like them to think that we're any kind of manufactured band, that we don't make our own decisions and we don't make our own music. To me that is everything that I'm passionate about, that we've created this whole thing from nothing. We decide everything."

When the critics discounted the band, which happened often, the band shrugged it off. "When I see criticism of us," Dumont told Mike Boehm of the *Los Angeles Times* in February, 1997, "a lot seems to be the kind where people see a pretty blonde girl and can't think there's anything of any depth there. I think that's a bias. [The album] is a snapshot of a suburban female in the '90s, and there are a lot of honest, heartfelt things she's singing about."

Critics may not have been interested in the band, but the public certainly was. By November "Don't Speak" hit #1 and #2 respectively on *Billboard's* Hot 100 airplay and Modern Rock chart. By the second week of December, *Tragic Kingdom* reached Billboard's #1 spot, which it would hold on to for nine weeks.

No Doubt was now headlining theater shows, which were selling out, all over the world. The constant touring was a blast—they'd played nearly every night since the beginning of '96—but by the fall of that year, they needed a break. Although the band members were coming to terms with their lead singer's star turn, everyone was tired and tempers were running short. In addition, Stefani was having problems with her vocal chords. They canceled and postponed a few shows here and there to give her a voice a rest, but soon realized that she needed more than an occasional break. They canceled a European tour scheduled for the month of November so that Stefani could recuperate.

Dumont described the band's realization with *Liner Notes* magazine just a few months later, in January, 1997: "We had been touring so hard so when Gwen had the throat problems, it forced us to stop a couple of times. There was a point where we thought we may never be able to tour again like this. Maybe some one-off shows here or there and for us that was such a hard thought because we always wanted to be a road band—a live band—that was always our first love. I mean Gwen cried all the time about it. She was really upset. Fortunately, she's working with a vocal coach and we're out here and it's working. This tour, she's fine. We take it at a little slower pace. We have humidifiers everywhere on the bus and I think we're going to be fine. It's scary. We thought from then on maybe we'd be just a recording band, who knows."

By December, No Doubt was performing again, apparently the rest and Stefani's work with her vocal coach paid off. On December 7, the band played their most recent hits, "Don't Speak" and "Excuse Me Mr." on *Saturday Night Live*. They quickly stepped up to full-length gigs, with no ill affects.

In a review of their December 12, 1996 show at Convention Hall in Asbury Park, NJ, *Rolling Stone's* concert reviewer had nothing but praise for the band's performance:

"The band's recent time off from touring—due to Stefani's vocal chord problems—hasn't killed No Doubt's explosive live energy. Far from it, the ska-influenced Orange County, California band is exhausting to watch. Bassist Tony Kanal and guitarist Tom Dumont (who now sports platinum blonde hair) leap and skank all night with breaks only for guitar changes. Drummer Adrian Young is plain acrobatic on the set, while horn players Gabriel McNair and Phil Jordan try to out-jump each other during the hyperactive numbers. Stefani, of course, is unstoppable-kicking, jumping, climbing to the top of the speakers. She's a one woman wrecking ball."

CHAPTER EIGHT

Different People

With Gwen's vocal chords back in shape, No Doubt started the next leg of their tour in early 1997. It was now just a little over a year since *Tragic Kingdom* was released, and they had graduated to headlining stadium venues. In January they attended the American Music Awards, they were nominated for the AMA Favorite New Artist for Pop or Rock. In February they performed "Spiderwebs" at the Grammy Awards. They were nominated for two awards, Best Rock Album and Best New Artist. They didn't bring home any awards that spring, but the band, on the cusp of celebrating its tenth anniversary—their first official gig had been in March of 1987—was happy just to have been nominated.

Although at this point she still lived at home (on the rare occasions No Doubt was in town), Stefani finally felt like she'd grown up. "I love being 27," she told the *Face Magazine's* Jonathan Bernstein later that spring.

"Because I grew up in a family that was so perfect in its way of being traditional—church every Sunday and four kids and we all get along—I was always in this little nest. I always felt like a kid forever. Now I finally feel like I have my own life. It's got a lot to do with the fact that I was away all the time, and they're at home, and I finally have accomplished something. I feel at this age and at this time in my life, that I'm finally doing what I'm supposed to do."

She'd be doing a lot more of it too, as the band continued its hectic schedule through the end of the year. On April 11, No Doubt performed the fifth single to be released off of *Tragic Kingdom,* "Sunday Morning," on the *Tonight Show.* The song, despite its upbeat reggae riffs, was again about the Kanal/Stefani break up. Along with those of "Happy Now" and "Hey You," "Sunday Morning's" lyrics were the most overtly angry and bitter songs Stefani had penned.

You're on the other side of the mirror / So nothing's looking quite as clear / Thank you for turning on the lights / Thank you, now you're the parasite / I didn't think you had it in you / And now you're looking like I used to!

Again, the songs were written collaboratively, and Kanal, along with Stefani's brother Eric, developed the music. In the "Hub Interview" Kanal described the scene on the day they came up with the initial licks that would eventually turn into their fifth hit. Gwen was over at Kanal's house, and they were messing around with chords, trying to come up with an idea. At some point, Stefani, became really ill and locked herself in the bathroom to get sick. While she was in there, Kanal serenaded her from the hallway. The band claims that the song is Kanal's favorite.

The video for "Sunday Morning" seems to present a day in the life of the band at work and play, circa 1993, about the time Kanal was splitting with Stefani and Eric was disengaging from the band. The narrative is simple. The band finishes up a rehearsal in the backyard garage of the band's Beacon Street house. Stefani, looking '40s-fabulous in a black sweater and matching leopard-print skirt and shoes, leaves to get groceries, then returns. Meanwhile, the rest of the band starts cooking a meal and setting a picnic table out back. Everyone seems to be getting along, having lots of fun, but there are moments where you detect a palpable undercurrent of tension between Kanal and Stefani, as well as one semi-hallucinogenic scene of an outburst of anger from Stefani. But everything quickly turns back to normal. After the picnic gets underway, the scene ends with a massive food fight. Eric, dressed in a suit, is in all of the backyard scenes, observing the band, but staying uninvolved.

Aside from releasing the biographic video, No Doubt landed another feature article in *Rolling Stone,* and to everyone's delight, the cover of the May issue included the entire band. The stylist dressed everyone in white surgical garb, either to signify the equality of the band members or perhaps to signal the start of the summer fashion season.

The perks of fame became readily apparent to the band that summer. Not only did George Lucas, with daughter in tow, visit with the band backstage at one of their Northern California gigs, but Tony's biggest musical influence, Prince, caught a show they played in Minneapolis.

As the band continued to tour, they were getting ever more encouraging news about the progress of their album sales. By the summer of 1997, *Tragic Kingdom* had sold seven million copies in the U.S. and eleven million worldwide. And, while nowhere close to the numbers of their sophomore effort, *No Doubt* climbed to sales of 250,000.

Their September MTV Video Music Awards' Best Group Video win for "Don't Speak" kicked off another stellar season. During another European tour, the band stopped in to visit their friend George Lucas while they were in London and got to watch the filming of a *Phantom Menace* fight scene.

For the last leg of the *Tragic Kingdom* tour, the band traveled all over the world. In Singapore, the band had to obey strict laws for public performances—Stefani's mother certainly would have approved—no

swearing allowed. They also hit cities in South America and India. Tony's parents flew out for the India leg of the tour, and his extended family attended their shows.

They wrapped up the year with multiple releases. Interscope released the *Beacon Street Collection* as part of their back catalogue. And the band's first live performance video also came out. *Live in the Tragic Kingdom* was filmed in the band's backyard at Anaheim's Arrowhead Pond Arena. Coincidentally, the Disney Corporation owned the arena, and was the subject of the album's title song, which lamented the lost ideals of the company's visionary founder, Walt Disney.

The band experienced a phenomenal ride thanks to *Tragic Kingdom*: One album, five singles, multiple world tours, not to mention mulit-Platinum sales. Even as they were thick in the middle of their touring schedule, No Doubt was already looking forward to their follow-up album.

"We've got two years of experience touring around the world," Stefani told *Los Angeles Times* reporter Heidi Seigmund Cuda in May of 1997. "It seems like we could make an amazing record, but at the same time we haven't done it in so long, we're gonna just have to see what happens."

And despite several years of the rock 'n' roll dream: Screaming fans, fawning music-industry types, and constant media attention, they were keeping it all in perspective. "The fact that we even got this chance is like hitting the lottery," Stefani added.

"We have to remember that with our next record, everyone might hate us," Dumont said in the same interview. "So we're setting ourselves up mentally so we don't expect success. No one owes us anything."

CHAPTER NINE

Home

In January, No Doubt took a well-deserved break. The band members left Orange County to take up residence in their respective L.A. rock-star digs, and at the age of twenty-nine, Gwen finally moved out of her parents place. The band relaxed, spent time with friends and family, soaked in the Southern California weather, and did all the things they'd missed while they were on the road.

In February, the band rented a place in the Hollywood Hills so that they could start work on their follow up. Kanal lived in the house, located on L.A.'s scenic and storied Mulholland Drive, the rest of the band had to commute. The band didn't know what kind of music they were going to write at the beginning of the process, but they were certain of two things: They wanted to explore stylistically and they wanted to take their time. Thanks to the multi-Platinum success of *Tragic Kingdom,* they had established enough clout with their label to do both.

"We said when we began it that if we were going to make another record, we had to do something we'd be really proud of," Stefani reflected in an interview with John Everson for the June 2000 issue of the *Illinois Entertainer.* "Something that would show the experience of our thirteen years together.

One of the most important aspects of the band was the diverse musical styles each member brought to the table. On *Tragic Kingdom,* they took tentative steps towards blending their ska-punk leanings with other influences. Their next album would again celebrate that diversity, but in a musically more mature, bolder way.

After more than a decade of performing and writing, Stefani's confidence had grown. According to the other band members, Stefani took the lead on the creative direction of the album. In an interview with Toure for the June 19, 2000 issue of *Rolling Stone,* Dumont and Young described Stefani's role:

"When we went into making this record, Gwen wanted to do music that wasn't as quirky," Dumont told Toure. "When a band pushes to be serious, there's this lame side to that idea. But that's the direction she was pulling us, and we all wanted to follow."

Lyrically, Gwen, as the singer, was used to pitching her ideas to the band. She didn't play an instrument, so in the past she deferred to Kanal, Dumont, and Young to develop instrumentation. Now, however, she was willing to throw her own ideas into the mix. "She has ideas all the time, and we don't," Adrian added during the discussion. "Even drum parts, though she sometimes doesn't know what she's talking about, but she sometimes does."

When Toure later posed the question to the singer, Stefani downplayed her role. "Am I the creative leader?" she said. "I don't know. But my opinion sure counts for a lot in my group of friends, and that feels good. I think I've earned that."

The songwriting process was still a collaborative effort. Generally they would start with either Stefani and Kanal or Stefani and Dumont hashing out the basics of a song that they would then bring to the rest of the band. At that point, they would still be fairly raw. Kanal described their working style for John Everson of the *Illinois Entertainer.* "They're bare and almost embarrassing, but we just riff off each other. You've got to open up. It's how we've always done it—it's a very organic starting point," Kanal said. "Then we bring it to the rest of the band. That's the hardest part—actually taking an acoustic idea and taking it to the band level. One thing that Adrian [Young, drummer] always does is make us try things with a different beat or a faster or slower tempo. We literally will go through ten different ways of playing the song until we find what makes sense."

The process was much the same as it was in the early days of the band, when Eric Stefani was the creative leader. Eric actually collaborated with the band on two songs recorded for *Return of Saturn*, "Staring Problem" and "Everything in Time." For the heavily ska-inflected "Staring Problem," the band sat together and each had to write a part in turn. "Staring Problem" made it on to the album, and "Everything in Time" was slated to be released as a B-side.

As collaborative as the process was, Stefani took the lead in generating ideas for lyrics. Many of those ideas came from journals she kept while on tour.

"It was a great help later in writing the album, because when you look back on what you've written, you don't even remember writing a lot of it," she told John Everson for the June 2000 issue of the *Illinois Entertainer*. "It's strange, but you really can write a song and not know what you're writing about until afterwards. Then it says so much more to you after it's written."

Stefani once again delved deep into her own experience for her subject matter. Her songs in *Tragic Kingdom* displayed the anger and pain of a young woman losing her first love. Her lyrics have grown up with her, and they're now more complex and subtle.

In these new songs she reflected on the changes in her life: Her confusion over the path she's chosen; her desire for marriage; and the joys, frustrations, and fears of her relationship with Gavin. Blonde bombshell or no, you think you'd feel secure about your relationship when you've seen groupies targeting the guys in your own band?

It would seem like a dream, but the match certainly had its ups and downs. It's hard to develop a relationship when both people are constantly on the road.

"I feel like it's hard for me to do more than one thing really good," she told the *Illinois Entertainer*. "Being in a band takes twenty-four hours a day, seven days a week of my passion. It takes a lot out of you and my relationships have suffered, because I'm not putting the time into them. And that's what my songs are about, really—I write about the stuff in my life that's off-balance. The past couple years were really my time to grow."

"When we made *Tragic Kingdom* I was twenty-three," Kanal reflected on Stefani's artistic development in the same interview. "Now I'm twenty-nine, Gwen's thirty. . .we're in a much different place in our lives now and I think it shows on the record. One thing about our band is what you see is what you get; we never try to manufacture, it's very sincere work. This is who we are. I think there's a certain sacrifice that we make in the kind of lyrics that Gwen writes. They're very honest and very sincere but you're giving away personal stuff. The virtue of that is you can really tell the songs are coming from us."

Stefani found that sitting down to write songs for the follow up, at one point tentatively titled, *Magic's in the Makeup* and later switched to *Return of Saturn*, was much harder than her last go-round. The process was harder, in part, because she wanted to become a better songwriter. "I was lost," she told Peter Davis in an interview for a 2002 issue of *Paper* magazine. "The making of that record was a growing phase. You can hear it in the songs. I didn't know how to write songs when I did *Tragic Kingdom*. I kind of figured it out. I really wanted to be a good songwriter. I wrote in my journal and cried. Ugggh! It was such a serious mood. You can see it in my style. I had pink hair, but I didn't know what I was doing. I was turning thirty and going through a weird phase."

It didn't help that she was also having a hard time adjusting after being on tour for so long. Life on the road was hectic and fast paced, and afforded little time to think, but it had become the norm. Now that she was back in Los Angeles, she had plenty of time to think about what her life had become and what her future was supposed to be. It was overwhelming. "We were in our own weird little world when we were on tour," Stefani told Aidin Vaziri in the April 12, 2000 issue of *Rolling Stone*. "Coming home, at first I thought I was fine, but then I slipped into this weird depression. I felt like I was going through some transition or growing pains."

That said, she gamely waded back into reality and started exploring what it had to offer. Thanks to the band's decision to take their time on the album, everyone in the band had the opportunity to enjoy a few side projects. In March, Young played drums for Orange County pop-punk-ska scene veterans The Vandals. Stefani had her share of extracurricular activities. In addition to making an appearance as a waitress in a Rufus Wainwright video (which was actually shot at her house), she sang two torch songs at a benefit for Don Henley's Walden Woods Foundation ("I Can Dream, Can't I" and Elvis Costello's "Almost Blue"). Later that year, former '80's rockabilly star and label mate (although it would be his last album on the Interscope label) Brian Setzer invited her to sing a duet for his album, *Dirty Boogie*. "You're the Boss" was originally performed by the onscreen and off-screen lovers Elvis and Ann Margret in the 1964 classic movie, *Viva Las Vegas*.

"I couldn't believe he even knew who I was!" she told John Everson in an interview for the *Illinois Entertainer*. "I told him, 'I wore poodle skirts in high school because of you!' But singing with him was just the easiest, most natural thing. I sang onstage with him one night when he played a show at The Greek and we had a party at my house afterwards. He's really seen it all—he knows what it's like to have success when you're so young and then to have it taken away."

Of course, there were numerous awards shows to attend. In September, Stefani—known as well for her outfits as for her singing prowess—wowed fans and photographers at the MTV Video Music Awards as she strode down the red carpet sporting a Smurf-blue faux fur bikini top with hair dyed to match.

No Doubt wrapped up the year by contributing a song for *The Rugrats Movie* soundtrack. They recorded "I Throw My Toys Around" with punk-new wave icon, Elvis Costello, who produced and co-wrote the song.

CHAPTER TEN

Waiting Room

No Doubt was true to their promise to themselves to take their time producing *Return of Saturn*. They had initially planned on working with Matthew Wilder, who produced *Tragic Kingdom* but midway through decided to look for another producer, which likely added to the time it took to create the album. Names were bandied about at length, and several producers worked on one-off tracks, but the band eventually settled on Glen Ballard, producer of Alanis Morissette's *Jagged Little Pill*, in February of 1999. One of the tracks off *Return of Saturn* made it out much earlier than the rest of the album.

"New," which was produced by Jerry Harrison, was the first song the band wrote after *Tragic Kingdom*. The song turned up on the soundtrack—released in March—for the indie movie, *Go,* and picked up a good amount of airplay.

"New" had a decidedly new wave sensibility. The song, with lyrics written by Stefani would be the first song to allude to her new relationship with Gavin. It's full of hope and trepidation:

oh you're different / you're different from the former / like a fresh battery / I'm energized by you

don't let it go away / this feeling has got to stay / and I can't believe I've had this chance now / don't let it go away.

The video they produced was something of a spy thriller, which starts with a car chase scene and ends up at a rave. Young and Dumont pursue Stefani, sporting pink hair, to the club. Tony, appearing as a mod maharajah, seems to be in cahoots with Stefani, but the story line is a bit vague.

By May, the band had recorded seventeen songs, which were mixed in July by Jack Joseph Puig (noted for his work with such bands as Jellyfish, the Goo Goo Dolls, and Tonic, among others) at L.A. studio, Ocean Way. They completed mixing in July, but pushed back a planned release to record a few more songs. According to *Rolling Stone,* Interscope sent the band back into the studio to come up with a "surefire" hit.

The band kicked off an eight-city West Coast club tour at the end of September. It would be a memorable tour. Not only did Gwen turn thirty on October 3, but six nights later, on the final night of the tour, at San Francisco's famed theater, The Fillmore, bandmate Young proposed to his girlfriend, Nina, onstage. They were married several months later in January, with the entire No Doubt family in attendance. Stefani served as bridesmaid to Nina, and Dumont and Kanal were groomsmen.

No Doubt released their first track from *Return of Saturn* that same month. The highly anticipated single, "Ex-Girlfriend" stayed on the alternative charts for twenty-seven weeks.

The song was a melting pot of musical styles. The first few bars of the song are world music contemplative, but the idea that this could be the next "Don't Speak" gets dispelled moments later when the song breaks into an aggressive punk, new wave snarl, and then at various points, the song slides into an R&B beat with Stefani rapping her lines. It was one of the last songs recorded for the album.

Young explained how "Ex-Girlfriend" ended up on *Return of Saturn.* "To me, it had a little bit of the old energy that we had in years previous, which seemed to be lacking a little bit on the record," Young told Launch Radio Networks in March 2000. "It just was, like, the last piece of the puzzle. It had energy, and it was kind of fast, and it had a little bit of an attitude to it—it was a little more on the *Tragic Kingdom* side of things because I think we lost a little bit of our innocence after all of our travels and getting older and becoming successful.

"And with 'Ex-Girlfriend,' it seems like we just stripped it down and said, 'Let's belt something out here.' And it happened to come out good."

In fact, the song marked a departure from the typical acoustic writing process the band had established. "We were really pushing ourselves to come up with one more up-tempo song for the album," Kanal told John Everson of the *Illinois Entertainer.*

"We'd already mastered a version of the record and thought we were done. But one day we went to Tom's house—he's got a little computer studio set-up—and we used the computer to make this soundscape. Then Gwen came in and worked on top of that. It was a very different process for us but it was fresh and exciting because we'd never done anything like that before." It was a process the band would return to on their next album.

There was plenty of speculation about the song, as most people surmised that it was about Kanal. The lyrics seemed to point in that direction:

I kinda always knew I'd end up your ex-girlfriend / I hope I hold a special place with the rest of them / And you should know it makes me sick to be on that list / But I should have thought of that before we kissed

After all, he was Stefani's ex. The song was actually about Gavin, but as the No Doubt singer was forced to assure everyone, they had not broken up.

The video, which was shot by Hype Williams, is visually aggressive as well. The colors are Technicolor bold, but with a slightly acidic tinge. Stefani's pink locks are braided, her makeup is couture garish, and her outfits run the gamut from punk-rock chick to gangsta hip. In the video, Stefani plays a spurned girlfriend-turned-hit man, who at the climax of the video—disguised in a sort of gangbanger-meets-Unibomber get up—beats up her ex and his bodyguards in a bathroom. At the conclusion, a cartoon aesthetic creeps into the video. Stefani and Kanal's characters, crash through the skyscraper window and zoom towards the street, still fighting.

Return of Saturn finally hit record shelves on April 11. It had been a long, grueling process, but one that No Doubt believed was worth the effort.

"We were not going to put a time limit on it—all of our records take really long," Stefani told the *Illinois Entertainer. "Tragic Kingdom* took us three years to create. The pressure of going into a studio and having to hurry up to get the next take can creatively be a good thing, but it was a nice luxury to go in and really work on every part in the studio for this record."

"We didn't think it would take two years to make—we figured six months to a year," Kanal added. "But looking back on it, I wouldn't change anything. We had to go through that process—stopping and starting and trying to push ourselves to write more and more songs."

Reviews in the press were, for the most part, positive. *Rolling Stone's* Barry Walters was particularly impressed with the album, as well as with the quartet's evolution as individual musicians: "The propulsion fathered by bassist Kanal and drummer Adrian Young now matches any rap-metal rhythm section's bluster," he wrote. "But it's never showy, always supportive, and Tom Dumont's guitar attack has similarly sharpened. At a time when chart bands risk few experiments, No Doubt present a kaleidoscope of vivid arrangements that can still kick butt.

Below its polished surfaces, *Return of Saturn* is bittersweetly conflicted; those contradictions underscore its purity of intent. No Doubt want to live up to their name and believe in themselves. Stefani's inability to do just that enables her to finally transcend the band's cartoon persona. No longer just a girl, this skanking flirt has finally grown into a woman."

Apparently the record-buying public agreed that their follow-up passed muster. A week after it was released *Return of Saturn* debuted at #2 on the *Billboard* Top 200 Chart.

The next single to go to radio was "Simple Kind of Life," which was completely different in tone from the two previous tracks. More in the vein of a folk/rock ballad, the song is the more mature "Don't Speak" of *Return of Saturn*. In "Simple Kind of Life," as in other tracks on the album, such as "Comforting Lie" and "Marry Me," Stefani lays out her dreams of the future: Marriage and children and tries to reconcile them to her current life.

The tone of "Simple Kind of Life" is vulnerable, sad, and rueful, and although it's clearly a personal statement about her own confusion, it's something that a lot of women, especially as they enter their thirties, can relate to. Getting into relationships and failing to realize when their partner is not intending to be there for marriage and feeling conflicted about wanting marriage and children while at the same time being concerned about losing their freedom.

For a long time I was in love / Not only in love, I was obsessed / With a friendship that no one else could touch / It didn't work out, I'm covered in shells / Now all the simple things are simply too complicated for my life / How'd I get so faithful to my freedom? / A selfish kind of life / When all I ever wanted was the simple things / A simple kind of life.

Sophie Muller, who's known for her work with the Eurythmics and Annie Lenox and who had also worked on "Don't Speak," directed the video for "Simple Kind of Life." Although Stefani is still in her pink hair period, the tone of the video is much softer than the jarring colors of "Ex-Girlfriend." It's a lush production, which swings between sorrowful and funny moods.

Some of the scenes depict Stefani (in a pink afro), wearing a wedding dress (which she and Muller designed, inspired by a John Galliano dress), running through a town with Young, Kanal, and Dumont (dressed as grooms) in pursuit. At one point there's a fantasy scene with hundreds of wedding cakes— the groomsmen are bashing them with baseball bats while Stefani at first looks on in horror, then desperately tries to pick up the remains of one of the frosting-laden victims. These scenes are interspersed with three scenes of Stefani interacting with each of her three bandmates as boyfriends. The funniest of these is the last: Stefani and Young are sitting on a couch, on the wall behind them is a huge circular, glowing birth control pack.

She sings the line, *I always thought I'd be a mom* , and there's no response from Young, but at her next line, *Sometimes I wish for a mistake,* he gives her a nervous glance. Again, with *The longer that I wait the more selfish that I get* , no response from Young. But as she slyly sings, *You seem like you'd be a good dad,* he gives her a look of terror and bolts from the couch.

What's great about both the song and the video is that they portray these very real emotions, but subtly point out their ironies as well.

After a series of press promotions in the U.S., Europe, Japan, and Australia, No Doubt kicked off the *Return of Saturn* tour in Dallas at the beginning of June. In between award shows (including the 2000 Teen Choice Awards, where No Doubt performed *Simple Kind of Life* complete with Stefani in "the" wedding gown) interviews, photo shoots, and the taping of their own VH1 *Storytellers*, they continued to perform. As hectic as it was, Stefani was excited to get back into the thick of things.

"Being on tour is not real life, you know?" she told John Everson for the June 2000 issue of *Illinois Entertainer* magazine. "It's fantasy life. Nothing's really real. There are loads of people who love you for the moment. The whole tour life is so surreal, but it's awesome. Reality was nice for awhile, but I'm ready to go back to fantasy!"

Kanal agreed. "There's something beautiful about being able to play clubs and have that very intimate energy being shared between the audience and the performers. But there's also something great about being able to get onstage and look out at an arena and play for 15,000 people. That's rock 'n' roll. It's addicting."

The fantasy was indeed in full gear, as was the band's fast-paced schedule. At the beginning of September, they shot the video for "Bathwater." "Bathwater" came back to No Doubt's two-tone roots, mingled with the suggestion of a Broadway musical. Stefani loved musicals as a kid, and although *Annie* had a few sassy numbers, "Bathwater" seems closer in spirit to saltier productions along the lines of *Chicago* or *Gentlemen Prefer Blondes.*

As a matter of fact, in the video Stefani once again looks to the past for hair-do ideas, this time choosing Marilyn Monroe as her model. They once again selected Sophie Muller to direct, but the similarities to "Simple Kind of Life" ended there. They also brought in Fatima Robinson, who's worked with Michael Jackson, Dr. Dre, Mary J. Blige, and the Backstreet Boys, among others, to choreograph the video. It's a tongue-in-cheek dance video, which draws on early elements of the genre. There are obvious nods to break dancing and the movie *Flashdance,* and, with the phrase "Can't Touch This," emblazoned on Stefani's halter top, a visual reference to MC Hammer.

Set to a sexy, brassy beat, the lyrics pose the eternal question women ask of men in demand in general (and Stefani seemed to be asking Rossdale in particular): With all these writhing beauties throwing themselves at you, why have you chosen me, and why am I allowing myself to fall for you?

Wanted and adored by attractive women / Bountiful selection at your discretion / I know I'm diving into my own destruction / So why do we choose the boys that are naughty? / I don't fit in so why do you want me? I know I can't tame you. . .but I just keep trying.

Kanal had gotten used to the experience of his personal life laid bare before the public by this point. "I would never try to censor her art and she would never do that with me," Kanal reflected during a conversation with John Everson for the *Illinois Entertainer.* "I think the songs are general enough that they aren't about "Gwen and Tony" or about "Gwen and her new relationship." I think anyone can relate to these songs, anyone who's been in a relationship of any sort. . .It's kind of a very public therapy. But it's art, it's real. Sometimes you have to go through a little pain to get something special."

For new boyfriend Rossdale it would still take some getting used to. In an interview for the November 2, 2001 issue of *Rolling Stone* magazine, Christina Saraceno asked whether Stefani "pretty much lays things on the line in her lyrics."

Rossdale responded, "She certainly does. She certainly does, I'm like, 'Can't you like, put a bit of poetry around that? I don't know—does it have to be that?' But that's her thing."

But as she admitted to *Details,* "If I get a crush on someone, that's that. My whole life is directed around that. I can't help it. I love love."

Her thoughts may have been focused solely on Rossdale, but she managed to keep a handle on the many events that were dictating her time. After wrapping up the "Bathwater" video shoot, and doing more interviews and shows, the band taped voiceovers for the animated TV series, *King of the Hill.* And Stefani finished up another project initiated over a year earlier. She and Moby shot the video for the soon-to-be hit "South Side."

"Working with Gwen was wonderful," Moby told Peter Davis in an interview for *Paper* magazine. "When she first came to the studio, I expected her to be a larger-than-life rock star, but she was so sweet and down-to-earth. It was the same when we worked on the "South Side" video. She has this very focused work ethic that is impressive, and she's a lot of fun to be around."

After the "South Side" video wrapped, No Doubt headed to Japan and Australia for a month to perform. When they returned in November, the publicity carousel continued to spin: Appearances on *Late Night with David Letterman* and MTV's *Total Request Live*, a photo shoot for the cover of *YM,* presenting awards at the Billboard Music Awards, live performances at the Radio Music Awards in Las Vegas, the VHI My Music Awards, and finally, KROQ's Almost Acoustic Christmas.

The band was everywhere. Perhaps because the band was together for so long before fame hit, they were able to maintain a sense of humility and perspective about their stardom. Their egos remained firmly in check, and their friendships remained intact.

In an interview with Mar Yvette for the December 2001 issue of *Mean Street* magazine, Stefani and Dumont discussed their fame and the enduring bond among the band members.

"As far as all the fame and celebrity stuff, that really is a strange part," Stefani said. "But it doesn't really soak in. It doesn't enter the real world of four best friends who make music together and get to have this extended childhood and go around dancing onstage for people. We feel very, very blessed to be doing this still. Everything after *Tragic Kingdom* has just been borrowed time. None of us expected that we'd still be doing this, you know?"

"The cool thing about all the fame and stuff after *Tragic Kingdom* is that we're still here and we still have the same friendships and still enjoy being together," Dumont added. "It's cool that we've made it without hating each other or becoming drug addicts or anything bad, you know what I mean? The analogy I use is that we're like brothers and sister. There are moments when we drive each other crazy, but at the same time we're really tight and have this deep connection. No matter what I do to piss off Tony today, tomorrow we're gonna be hanging out drinking and playing tennis."

CHAPTER ELEVEN

Rock Steady

A fter almost a year of promoting *Return of Saturn,* which, at the end of the year was still on the charts and had sold about 1.3 million copies, they were ready to sit down and start work on a new album. *Return of Saturn* was a self-conscious effort. It was the product of a group of people trying to grow as artists and to prove themselves as serious musicians.

Their goals for their next album were very different. No Doubt had arrived, and they wanted to enjoy their status. They had only two objectives in mind: Shake things up and have some fun.

One of the inspirations for *Rock Steady* was the music they'd been dancing to during post-performance parties on the *Return of Saturn* tour.

"We found this music called dancehall, which is a Jamaican [type of] music that's basically the evolved, modern version of ska [and] reggae," Stefani explained to Mar Yvette in the December 2001 issue of *Mean Street* magazine. "And that's what we've always loved. I mean, we started our band as a ska band. So when we started making this record we said, 'Let's make a record that we can dance to 'cause we wanna be in a club and hear our song come on.' So we just sat down and started writing and ended up recording in Jamaica with legendary Sly and Robbie, Steely and Clevie and just these hard-core dancehall producers. We had a real magical time there and it just set up the whole vibe for the record."

In addition to wanting to return a sense of fun to their work, or perhaps even to help them get back to that place, the band decided that, after so many years they needed to open up their creative process by inviting other collaborators into the mix.

"We've never written with other people," Stefani told Austin Scaggs of *Rolling Stone* in May, 2001, just as they had gotten underway. "We wanted to get in a room and see what kind of cultural collisions happened. I want this record to be short, simple, fun, and danceable."

It was a big step for the band, which had been determined from their earliest history to control their own sound. "We agreed that if there was any cool opportunity to write with other people we'd do it—not even to be on the album but for the life experiences," Stefani told Kieran Grant in 2002 for an article on the Canadian entertainment Web site, *Jam.canoe.ca.* "It used to be about not letting anyone into our world, which is foolish because you can learn so much."

No Doubt ended up working with multiple producers, in part because they wanted to get a variety of sounds and attitudes on the album, and in part because the producers they wanted to work with had limited time to spare to work with them. Production credits on *Rock Steady* read like a who's who guide to star producers: Jamaican producers Sly & Robbie and Steely and Clevie; Timbaland and the Neptunes who have produced Missy Elliott and Aaliyah, among others; Nellee Hooper, who's worked with Madonna and Bjork; William Orbit, known for his work with Madonna; Prince; Dave Stewart of the Eurythmics; and Ric Ocasek of the Cars.

"If there's one thing our success has afforded us, it's the opportunity to work with all these people that we've looked up to," Kanal told Jon Wiederhorn and Rebecca Rankin for MTV News. "We've listened to their music for so long and been so inspired by them. Hearing the stories these guys have to tell you is incredible," he added. "Ric told us amazing stories about Bad Brains and when he recorded *Rock for Light,* and that was so awesome. The energy and experiences these people have had is invaluable and it really rubs off on you."

Orbit produced "Making Out," Ocasek handled the new wave-heavy "Don't Let Me Down" and "Platinum Blonde Life, Hooper produced multiple tracks, including "Running," Steely and Clevie did "New Friend" and "Start the Fire," and Sly and Robbie produced two of the three hits off the album, "Underneath It All," and "Hey Baby." Timbaland and the Neptunes produced the other hit, "Hella Good."

Prince added tracks and produced "Waiting Room," a song that the band originally wrote for *Return of Saturn*, but chose not to include on the earlier album. "It's got all these crazy melodies," Stefani told Gavin Edwards in the October 16, 2001 issue of *Rolling Stone.* "It's so good. He's [Prince] such a genius. We played it for somebody from the record company, and they couldn't believe that we had that track in our back pocket." The collaboration may have been inevitable, Edwards commented. "Stefani says that when she first started dating Kanal in high school, "Tony thought he was Prince."

The collaborations were a measure of how far they'd come—they were getting serious talent to work on their album. No Doubt was very aware of just how privileged they were and the degree to which these outside contributions added to the final product.

Stefani and Dumont discussed their impact on the creative experience, as well as the final product with Mar Yvette in the December 2001 issue of *Mean Street* magazine. "Can you imagine if we just said, 'Nah, we're not gonna let anyone inside our world.'" Stefani mused. "This record was all about letting people into the No Doubt world and I think it reflects it."

Dumont agreed. "It's kind of like going to music school 'cause we're sitting with people like Prince and watching how they work and learning from them. Or working with Dave Stewart on "Underneath It All" was literally just us and a guitar for a half an hour and [coming] up with this really pretty, sweet song with a reggae vibe. When you collaborate, you're filtering your creativity through someone else's sensibility, so you come up with a different result than you would if you were just working by yourself."

There were other innovations in their creative process aside from bringing in outside collaborators. Before *Return of Saturn,* their writing process had been exclusively acoustic. On that album, they used ProTools, a digital editing program, to create the soundscape they played around with to write "Ex-Girlfriend, the final track written for the album. It was a fast, simple, and fun way to write a song, and the band returned to it as their starting point for their next album. "It opened us up creatively in this amazing way because it was just us being creative all day long with a microphone," Dumont told Mar Yvette in an interview for the December 2001 issue of *Mean Street.* "When we had about six or seven songs we were like, let's go to Jamaica and record these things. Then we came back and recorded more at my house again and when we had about fifteen songs that we really loved, we went to England to record them and we were done. That's how this album came about: Writing and recording in bits and pieces with things that were exciting and inspiring to us."

"It's easy to move music around with Pro Tools—we just brought down the disks," Kanal told Gavin Edwards in the November 16 issue of *Rolling Stone.* Their first stop was Port Antonio, Jamaica. "We would spend every morning drinking rum and Cokes or Red Stripes for breakfast, to get our heads in the right space. It's a wonder we got stuff done."

Using the computer as a jumping off point also let the band experiment with synth instrumentation and effects. "As far as the electronic thing, it didn't happen on the whole record, but it did on a lot of the record," Dumont told *Mean Street* magazine. "It's kind of me and Tony, deciding out of our own tastes, to lay down our instruments to experiment with keyboards. We just got a bunch of synthesizers and started messing around with making songs that way. So like on 'Hey Baby' Tony played half the bass line on the keyboard, and all these weird Star Wars sounds and laser noises that you hear were just us having fun with it. Right now, for me, using all these new elements to push music forward is really exciting."

No Doubt weren't the only ones casting about for a new musical partner that spring. In March, rap star Eve invited Stefani to contribute vocals to the track "Let Me Blow Ya Mind," for her upcoming album, *Scorpion.* The song was a crossover hit, reaching #1 on the Top R&B/Hip Hop Chart and #4 on the *Billboard* 200. In between Stefani's recording schedule, the duo performed the song live a handful of times that spring and summer, on *Saturday Night Live,* the First Annual BET Awards, and the 2001 Teen Choice Awards.

"I'm so lucky people ask me," Stefani told Peter Davis in an interview for *Paper* magazine in 2002. "The song with Eve had the most impact on me. I'd never worked with a rapper. Doing the video, it was like stepping into a whole other world. I love the idea of different worlds coming together. It was what ska was all about in the first place. And I got exposed to a whole other audience. Even just walking around New York, people who I didn't think would know who I am were like, 'Hey, what's up?'"

By August, No Doubt had finished most of their recording sessions with their army of producers. They headed back to London to record the title track and to hang out while Mark "Spike" Stent, the much-sought after mixer—whose client list includes U2 and Madonna, among many others—made sonic sense of their polyglot tapes. Or, as he described it for Gavin Edwards in the October 16, 2001 issue of *Rolling Stone,* "I've been helping them put together all the different styles, and putting the icing on the cake." Stefani knew Stent from his previous work with Rossdale's band, Bush.

The band kept their mind off pre-release jitters by contributing a remake of disco-queen Donna Summer's "Love to Love You Baby" for the soundtrack of Ben Stiller's model/thriller spoof, *Zoolander.* On her own, Stefani accepted awards on behalf of Moby and Eve at the MTV Music Video Awards and made the cover of *Blender* as one of the Fifty Sexiest Artists of All Time, as well as

Vanity Fair for their music issue. She also participated in an all-star version of Marvin Gaye's classic, "What's Going On," which was originally slated to be released on December 1, 2001 in honor of World AIDS Day, but was released to radio and MTV in mid-September to honor the victims of the September 11 terrorist attacks.

No Doubt went on tour with U2 the third week of October. Their first date was New York City's Madison Square Garden. Stefani described the experience in a post to the No Doubt Web site a month later. "The show couldn't have been more intense," she wrote. "The energy of the city coming together after the tragedies of September 11th was gorgeous. I really felt lucky to be there with my best friends offering our music as a way to heal and distract from the confusion and pain of these times. Seeing U2 under normal circumstances is emotional enough, but with the combination of their music and a city in mourning, the words of the songs took on a whole new meaning. By the end of the concert everyone in the audience was in tears." Instead of taking the next night off, No Doubt played a free show for area fans.

Even without the added emotional dimension of the recent tragedy, touring with U2 was an intense experience for No Doubt. Stefani describes U2's music as having been the soundtrack to their lives throughout high school and college, As Stefani confessed to *Teen Vogue* several months later, even though they were sharing the stage with the Irish rockers, they couldn't help feeling star struck.

"Tony and I were in the pit at the U2 concert after we opened for them," she recalled "And we were standing on the side and Bono was coming down the catwalk, and he saw us, and he reached down and held our hands, and sang to us, and I felt like a kid, like a total geek."

Their first single had been released a few weeks before they went on the road with U2. "Hey Baby," a funky, infectious, dancehall number, which features a mid-song rap interlude by Jamaican dancehall DJ Bounty Killer, was produced by No Doubt and veteran reggae production team Sly & Robbie. The song, written from Stefani's perspective, describes the singer's nightly amusement with the backstage antics of her bandmates and the determined groupies who pursue them.

I'm the kind of girl that hangs with the guys / Like a fly on the wall with my secret eyes / Takin' it in, try to be feminine / With my makeup bag watchin' all the sin.

DJ Bounty Killer's lines mimic the guys' maneuverings:

When you rock your hips you know that it amazes me / Got me off the hook and nuttin' else don't phase me / Can you be my one and only sunshine lady / If no, maybe, hey baby.

For their part, Dumont and Kanal (Young at this point was already married), embraced the song. In an interview with MTV News' Jon Wiederhorn and Rebecca Rankin just after its release, Kanal quipped, "It's actually a very PG version of the actual debauchery that goes on backstage."

"Well, you hate to turn [the girls] down and hurt their feelings," added Dumont.

The video, which premiered at the beginning of November, was shot in Los Angeles by Dave Meyers, who's directed videos for Missy Elliott, Mick Jagger, Jennifer Lopez, Ja Rule, and Pink, among others.

The exuberant video mirrors the humor of the song. Stefani dances, observes, rolls her eyes, and laughs at her rock 'n' roll boys while they run wild backstage: Pranks, gambling, brawling, and picking up babes. The video, enhanced with CGI animation is visually rambunctious as well, with garish colors, inventive camera effects, jerking shots of party scenes, and backdrops alternating between floating words and houndstooth patterns.

On the strength of "Hey Baby," *Rock Steady* debuted in *Billboard*'s Top 10. The CD was flying off the shelves, and critics liked it too. A month after its released, Rob Scheffield compared *Rock Steady* to its predecessor. " But while the album was heartfelt and subtle, it was a little overcooked. *Rock Steady* is looser and friskier. . ."

Scheffield approved of the change. "As you'd expect from titles like "Hella Good," "Hey Baby" and "Start the Fire," the music on *Rock Steady* is simple and propulsive, which in the time-honored rock 'n' roll manner forces the songs to improve; chord changes and turns of phrase that would have obfuscated themselves to death on *Return of Saturn* have no choice here but to get hot or go home."

"*Return of Saturn* was one of those records that was really labored, it was drawn-out way too long and overthought," Stefani said in an interview with Kieran Grant for the Canadian entertainment Web site, *jam.canoe.ca*. "Not in a negative way—we had to do that to get to this point. We had to go through a hard time to be able to sit in a room together and write fun songs. . ."

"You couldn't play *Return of Saturn* at a party," Dumont acknowledged in an Oct 16, 2001 *Rolling Stone* article written by Gavin Edwards. *Rock Steady* was a return to the upbeat mood of *Tragic Kingdom*. The album replete with the what Dumont described as "Star Wars noises and Devo-y bleeps" was a dance record. The underlying dancehall beat was energetic, fun, and sexy.

"These are songs you can really dance to—we were out dancing a lot when we made the record," Stefani told Tom Moon in the March 8, 2002 issue of *Rolling Stone*. "The mood is just so up, energetic, and that dancehall beat is the sexiest beat. I think this is probably our sexiest music."

The new groove was having an effect on Stefani—or perhaps it was the other way around—in her dress, performances, and attitude. She was beginning to embrace the idea that other people thought she was sexy. She discussed the new attitude with Neil Strauss in an interview for the January 31, 2002 issue of *Rolling Stone*."Yeah, the record does have a sexiness and a hipness that we've never had before," she said. "The thing about the sexy side, for me, is that I earned it. It wasn't until I felt comfortable wearing high heels, because when you're on heels—dude, you should try it—all of a sudden you're sexy. I finally feel like there's a side to me like, 'I'm a woman now,' which is fine."

Rock Steady was a marked shift from previous albums. If you heard "Hey Baby" without knowing who it was, No Doubt would not be your first guess. The band wasn't sure who their audiences would be that following year.

"I have no idea what the audience is going to be like," Stefani told Moon, "At least I know this much: We'll be playing to some people who never heard of No Doubt before "Hey Baby." We've gotten to be so many different kinds of bands—we were a garage band, then a ska band, then a punk band. When we started playing more than just ska, the ska people said, 'You're over.' I'm sure we lost people, but we picked up some new people too. And then when *Tragic Kingdom* happened, with every single it was a totally different audience. We don't discriminate. We're not the cool band, and people who like us are not the cool people."

The band didn't have too much time to worry about their new fan base. They wrapped up their tour with U2 at the end of November, but their schedule was still busy. Gwen picked up a few more accolades before the year ran out: She was named CosmoGirl of the Year and picked up the My Favorite Female Artist Award at the 2001 My VH1 Music Awards. Among other appearances, No Doubt performed at the Billboard Music Awards and, in their last performance of the year, on *Saturday Night Live*.

"It's just such a magical year," Stefani commented in an interview at the end of the year with Neil Strauss for the January 31, 2002 issue of *Rolling Stone*. "It's sad, because I know we're going to have a crash landing at some point, because we're just riding so high. Touring to me is becoming harder. The physical part of it is hard, the traveling part is hard, being away from people you love is getting harder and harder."

CHAPTER TWELVE

𝔐𝔞𝔯𝔯𝔶 𝔐𝔢

S tefani wouldn't be landing anytime soon. On the morning of New Year's Day, 2002, Rossdale proposed. It wouldn't be the simple life she envisioned growing up, but they would figure out a way to make the complications work. They'd been dating for six years by this point, so they had plenty of experience working through the issues particular to a long distance relationship between two hardworking rock stars.

"Any relationship is hard, but there are definitely things that are good and bad about ours," Stefani told *Teen Vogue* that spring. "Because we both do the same thing we understand exactly what the other is going through, but because we're so passionate about what we do, that passion takes up a lot of time. So the separation sometimes can be good because we can be creative and just focus on ourselves. But as the years go by we both think it sucks being apart. We'd prefer to be together, and our lives are more balanced when we're together."

Engagement or no, they wouldn't have much time to spend together for the foreseeable future. As difficult as it was, Stefani wasn't complaining about either her time away from Rossdale or the hard work she invested in the band.

"It's been a lot of hard work and we're reaping the rewards of that being able to get married," she told Kieran Grant for the Web site, *jam.canoe.ca*. "Being in a band that's like a family, being in a band with the same people for fifteen years, is a real commitment. Marriage is going to be the same kind of work. You get so much out of it."

Before kicking off their official *Rock Steady* tour in March, No Doubt made a few live appearances, including MTV Mardi Gras, along with Outkast. Drummer Young was noticeably absent at these appearances—he was anxiously awaiting the birth of his first child. His wife Nina gave birth to Mason James Young on February 9. At the end of February, Eve and Gwen picked up a Grammy for "Let Me Blow Ya Mind," and the band geared up for their tour by performing at a benefit concert for the Recording Artists Coalition.

No Doubt kicked off the *Rock Steady* tour in Puerto Rico's capital, San Juan. They took time off to shoot the video for their next single, "Hella Good." The track was a heavy metal, punk, and funk hybrid of an upbeat partying love song.

Your performance deserving a standing ovation / And who would have thought it'd be the two of us / So don't wake me if I'm dreaming / 'Cause I'm in the mood come on and give it up

You got me feeling hella good / So let's just keep on dancing / You hold me like you should / So I'm gonna keep on dancing.

Mark Romanek who's known for his work with Nine Inch Nails and Madonna directed the video. In the video, shot in black and white, No Doubt cavort in and around a sunken vessel off the coast of their old stomping grounds of Long Beach, California. Playing semi-aquatic, post-apocalyptic oddball versions of themselves, they hunt each other down through watery passageways, speed around on jet skis, perform, and generally have a good time.

No Doubt also had a few other items on their agenda to take care of before they started the European leg of their tour. They performed "Hella Good" and their upcoming single, "Underneath It All," on *Late Night* with Conan O'Brien. After contributing voiceovers to the video game, Malice (Stefani lent her voice to the title character), the band performed at Jay Leno's summer outdoor performance space. The same night they appeared on Leno, Stefani had her bachelorette party. Apparently she had a hella good time, as she later wrote fans on No Doubt's Web site. "We looked at old photos, talked, laughed, and drank till we were sick! After that we all went out to a club and danced to Jamaican Dancehall. It all ended in tears and falling out of the limo into Gavin's arms in my front yard. . .Don't ask me what time that was. Those girls definitely gave me a night to remember or not to remember."

Although the bridal shower the following day was a bit rough, Stefani recovered in time to start shooting the video for their next single, "Underneath It All," just four days later.

The ska-inflected love song had a nice story behind its creation: Not only was it romantic, but it was an amazing learning experience for everyone involved. No Doubt was in the middle of working on another song on the album in Los Angeles, when Stefani was scheduled to leave to visit Rossdale in Great Britain. Instead of halting work, the band followed their lead singer to London, where they completed the song. While the band was in London, they visited Dave Stewart, who co-wrote the reggae inflected love song.

The genesis of the song came from Stefani, as she told Neil Strauss for the January 31, 2002 issue of *Rolling Stone,* which came out not long after Rossdale had proposed.

"The day before we went over there, I was in the park with Gavin, and I had been keeping a journal," she said. "And we were so in love, and I wrote that line, 'You're lovely underneath it all.' You know, like, 'After all the shit we've been through, you're a really good person. I really think I might like you.'"

From that sketch of a journal entry, Stewart and the band produced a song, which Stefani said was essentially written in ten minutes. It was an amazing experience for the entire band.

"There's such experience behind that simplicity," Dumont told Gavin Edwards of *Rolling Stone* later that year. "I would have way overthought those chord changes."

Sophie Muller directed the video. Aside from a brightly colored bike ride scene through a Jamaican landscape, the video focuses on Stefani as she undergoes a transformation from elaborate glamour girl to simple beauty.

They spent the summer performing, starting in Europe in mid-June and wrapping up in Asia towards the end of August. The band rounded out the summer by winning the Best Group Video and Best Pop Video for "Hey Baby," at the MTV Video Music Awards, which were held at Radio City Music Hall in New York.

Stefani then had ten days to relax before her wedding. Rossdale, like an increasing number of grooms-to-be these days, was in charge of plans for the wedding. Stefani and Rossdale actually had two marriage ceremonies. The first, performed by the Church of England, was held on September 14th at St. Paul's Church in London's Covent Garden. It was an intimate affair— 130 friends and family attended. Rossdale wore a tux and shades, their Hungarian sheep dog sported pink and purple flowers on his collar. Stefani wore a pale pink and ivory dress designed for her by friend and Christian Dior designer, John Galliano. "Gwen is an old-fashioned romantic at heart," Galliano told Lauren Waterman in an article on Stefani for the March 2003 issue of *Teen Vogue*. "We share a deep respect for tradition, yet also a love of breaking with convention. We wanted the effect to be dreamy, with a contemporary twist."

After a quick honeymoon on the island of Capri, the Rossdales (Stefani legally changed her name, but keeps her maiden name as her stage name) flew back to Los Angeles, where they had a private ceremony with a Catholic priest and Stefani's parents. On September 28, Interscope chairman Jimmy Iovine, threw an enormous, celebrity-studded wedding celebration at his Beverly Hills home. "I didn't know what level it was going to be at," Stefani later told *Paper* magazine's Peter Davis. "It was beyond! It was the most spectacular event I've ever been to. Everyone's mouth was on the floor. I didn't think I'd be emotional the second time around, but I was."

Stefani didn't have time to enjoy her newlywed status, but the busy singer took the separation in stride. "When we got married," she told Lauren Waterman that fall in an interview for *Teen Vogue*. "We promised we would be there for each other. So it's cool if we're apart now; we're going to be together forever. I'm totally with him in my heart."

The band hit the road again, touring the states with dates that included opening for the Rolling Stones, as well as playing with Garbage and the Distillers. The band wrapped up their tour with a few Southern California dates, at Long Beach arena and Arrowhead Pond in their hometown of Anaheim. The kicker was Anaheim mayor Tom Daly honoring the band by presenting them with a key to the city on KROQ's morning show, "Breakfast with Kevin and Bean." It was a good way to end a spectacular year.

CHAPTER THIRTEEN

Hella Good

As they headed into 2003, No Doubt had no particular plans for the future. "We'll do whatever feels right at the time," Stefani told Peter Davis in an interview with *Paper* magazine. "Right now, I don't think anyone feels inspired to write a record."

Stefani was sure of one thing during her interview with Davis—she was happy to be where she was. ". . .turning thirty has been so cool," she said. "I just want to live life."

With no agenda in place for their next project, Stefani, Kanal, Dumont, and Young were able to pull back on the schedule they'd been maintaining the previous year. That, of course, didn't mean that they were completely idle. The band played the Super Bowl on January 26. In addition to performing "Just A Girl," they accompanied Sting during his performance of the Police classic, "Message In A Bottle."

They also shot the video for their fourth single from *Rock Steady*, "Running." The song, produced by Nellee Hooper is a simple, but lush love ballad.

Be / Be the one I need / Be the one I trust most / Don't stop inspiring me / Sometimes it's hard to keep on running / We work so much to keep it going / Don't make me want to give up.

Shot in Laguna Beach, the video features the band playing on the beach. It's essentially a family photo album. Still photos and old footage of the band—dating back to its earliest years—are interspersed with the beach scenes, which look as if they were shot with an 8-millimeter camera.

Stefani was also back on the newsstand. *Teen Vogue* chose her as the covergirl for their inaugural issue.

In the accompanying article, the singer discussed her husband, No Doubt, and the fashion line she was preparing to launch later that fall.

But that was still in the future. The band, after being nominated multiple times over the years, finally received their first Grammy award, Best Pop Performance by a Duo or Group With Vocal for "Hey Baby." And in addition to performing a medley of "Underneath It All," and "Hella Good," with No Doubt, Kanal took part in a tribute to the late Joe Strummer, jamming with Bruce Springsteen, Elvis Costello, Dave Grohl, Steve Van Zandt, and Pete Thomas on The Clash's "London Calling." No Doubt, excited about their win, played a club show at New York City's Hammerstein Ballroom. Gavin, along with members of Incubus, made a guest appearance with the band.

After Stefani gave the induction speech for The Police at the Rock and Roll Hall of Fame induction ceremony on March 10th, the band took a well-deserved break.

In September, the band got back together to record a cover of Talk Talk's "It's My Life," for their soon to be released greatest hits collection, *The Singles 1992-2003*. Nellee Hooper, who had produced their very new wave ballad, "Running," on *Rock Steady*, was back in the big chair on this track.

September 8th also saw the official premiere of Stefani's fashion label, L.A.M.B. The Fall 2003 collection, produced in partnership with LeSportsac included limited-edition bags and accessories. Many of the pieces were made from black rip-stop nylon covered words and phrases in a white gothic font. The handles resembled guitar straps. The L.A.M.B. bags jumped off the shelves immediately, and could be seen on the shoulders of fashionistas and celebrities alike. The full line of ready-to-wear clothing would come out in the spring, and the response boded well for Stefani's newest endeavor.

The emergence of her own fashion label was fate. Growing up, Stefani learned to sew from her mother. For much of her life, either she or her mother made her clothes. As she got busier with her music, she began making clothes with her stylist, Andrea Lieberman. They were making so many pieces that they decided to start their own clothing line. "We were going to do something really small and just sell our stuff at a few boutiques," Stefani told *Cosmopolitan* magazine's Jennifer Kasle Furmaniak the following summer. "And then I met this guy who said he wanted to do a clothing line with me and pay for everything. The best part was he said I could do whatever I wanted creatively. I was like, Are you kidding me? Okay."

The name L.A.M.B. came from Stefani's nickname for her dog growing up, and Stefani decided to have the letters mean something, so *L* stands for Love, *A* for Angel, *M* for Music, and *B* for Baby. As she explained to Peter Davis in an interview for *Paper* magazine the previous year, " 'LAMB' is anything cute," she said. "It's basically the clothes I wear. I want it to be my style, so I can wear them. I don't know what it will evolve into. I don't know if people will like it or not. I don't know anything about fashion. I'm still learning. It's just another creative thing for me to do, and it's exciting." L.A.M.B. would launch the full ready-to-wear line for sale in Spring 2003.

Stefani reconnected with the band in mid-October to shoot the video for "It's My Life." They chose noted photographer/director David LaChapelle, who they'd worked with previously on photo shoots, to direct. In the video, Stefani, playing a 1920s era vamp is on trial for the murders of three husbands, played by Dumont, Kanal, and Young.

The scenes alternate between Stefani committing the crimes, court room scenes, and Stefani struggling to escape her date with the electric chair.

Viewers may have thought her character was based on the Roxie Hart role in the movie *Chicago,* which had come out the previous year, but it's more likely that another vixen inspired the video's plotline. The video was shot at the historic Ambassador Hotel in Los Angeles. The hotel, which opened in 1921, was home to the famed Cocoanut Grove—Hollywood's nightclub to see and be seen in for decades, which figured prominently in a project Stefani had been working on during the band's summer break, the Martin Scorsese-directed bio pic, *The Aviator.*

In the movie, Leonardo DiCaprio plays Howard Hughes, the

eccentric billionaire aviation pioneer and Hollywood film producer, who was also famous for his romances with some of Hollywood's leading ladies. The movie covers his life from the late 1920s through the 1940s, the period when Hughes was directing and producing Hollywood films, most notably, *Hell's Angels,* and test flying aircraft he designed and produced.

Stefani played the part of Jean Harlow, who starred in *Hell's Angels.* That role not only catapulted Harlow from struggling actress to bona fide starlet status, but it transformed her into the platinum blonde siren who became Hollywood's first sex symbol.

Stefani only had two scenes in the movie. In Stefani's scenes, Harlow accompanies Hughes to the premiere of *Hell's Angels.* In one scene, the pair walk down the red carpet, besieged by photographers, reporters, and fans. They walk up to a podium, and Harlow thanks Hughes for including her in the picture. The other scene is very brief, during the screening of the movie, Hughes, seated next to Harlow, is crushing her hand in anticipation of the audience's reaction to the movie.

Stefani had been toying with the idea of trying to get a film role for several years, and had even gone on a few auditions. But the story of how she landed the role sounds like something out of an early movie screenplay. Leonardo DiCaprio retold the story in an interview for the special features segment, *A Life Without Limits: The Making of the Aviator.*

Scorsese had been looking for someone with "that quintessential '20s platinum blonde look" to play Harlow in the *Hell's Angels* premiere scenes. "He was driving down Sunset [Boulevard], as the story goes, and he saw Gwen Stefani on a billboard and said, who the hell is that? She looks just like Jean Harlow."

Or, as Scorsese himself put it, "Gwen Stefani is just literally Jean Harlow." The director and the cast were impressed not only with Stefani's physical resemblance to Harlow, but with her commitment to researching her role as well.

"She really did her research for the role," DiCaprio commented in the "Making of" documentary. "And I can't think of anyone who could have better portrayed Jean Harlow than she.

For her part, Stefani was thrilled to have landed the role, small as it was. "You can imagine how excited I was," Stefani commented. "I mean, she's obviously an idol of mine. She was the original blonde bombshell."

For Stefani, it was an amazing first step into filmmaking. If working with a series of top producers on *Rock Steady* the previous year was akin to going to music school, she was now enrolled in the Ivy Leagues of film making. Scorsese is known for his meticulously researched historical projects.

"When I went in to try out, he could've talked about Jean Harlow for the rest of the day; he knew everything about her," Stefani told Tom Lanham in an interview for *Wave.com.* "So you can tell when he works on a project, he explores every bit of it, so he has layers and layers to draw from, even if he doesn't use them."

If you're playing a Scorsese role, you become an expert on your character and their environment. Stefani took her cue from Scorsese and jumped into the research. The self-described girlie-girl brought an expertise of her own to the role and had just one beef on set: Her makeup.

"I would have done it a little differently," she told Jonathan Van Meter in an interview for the April 2004 of *Vogue.* "I'm always in control of my hair and makeup. I was like, 'Are you sure you want the lips to be that thin? Jean Harlow's were bigger than that. It's not like I didn't read two biographies and watch eighteen of her movies before I got here.' But what are you going to do? They were in control. I couldn't say anything. It was hard."

Stefani did have firm control over her music career, which was now well into its second decade. In November, she and her No Doubt cohorts celebrated their musical longevity with the release of three projects: Their first retrospective, *The Singles 1992-2003; Rock Steady Live;* a live concert DVD filmed at two shows in Long Beach during the 2002 Rock Steady Tour; and *Boom Box,* a two CD/two DVD box set featuring The Singles 1992-2003, Everything in Time (B-sides, Rarities, Remixes), The Videos 1992-2003 DVD, and the *Live in the Tragic Kingdom* DVD.

CHAPTER FOURTEEN

What Are You Waiting For?

A fter picking up their second Grammy award for Best Pop Performance By A Duo Or Group With Vocal for "Underneath It All," No Doubt took off the first half of 2004 to work on individual projects. Stefani's first order of business was doing publicity for L.A.M.B.'s Spring launch. It turned out that clothing design was in her blood.

"When I told my mother I was going to be on *Vogue,* she started crying," Stefani told Jonathan Van Meter in the interview for that April 2004 cover story. "She was looking through the designs in my book, and she got really emotional. My great-grandma used to start on New Year's day, which was her birthday, and she would sew every person in her family a quilt and, like, flannel pajamas and then the next Christmas you'd get it. Her daughter, my mom's mom, made every single thing my mother wore, to the point where she didn't get to choose her own clothes until she was, like, engaged. And then my mom made our clothes. I used to be kind of bummed. Like, 'Can't I go to the mall?'"

Occasional mall lust aside, Stefani loved to design and make clothes. She made her own prom dress, which was copy of Grace Kelly's dress from the Alfred Hitchcock movie *Rear Window.* Her onstage outfits were a combination of thrift-store finds and original creations fueled by frequent trips to the fabric store with her mother.

The L.A.M.B. collection included jeans, pants, blazers, blouses, halter tops, and skirts, as well as T-shirts and tank tops. The collection was available at such high-end retail stores as Barneys, Bergdorf Goodman, Henri Bendel, Fred Segal, Nordstrom's, and Saks Fifth Avenue. On line, in addition to *www.l-a-m-b.com* it was available at *shopbop.com,* which according to *People* magazine, counted among its customers celebrities Jessica Simpson, Hilary and Haylie Duff, Denise Richards, and Christine Taylor, as well "women who must have the most popular fashions, the moment they are available."

The line warranted coverage in the democratic how-to guides of *Lucky* to the haute couture heavy pages of *Elle* and *Vogue.*

That spring, Stefani also got to work on a solo recording project. Originally conceived as a fun, fast, and easy riff on '80's dance pop, the album steamrolled into a massive undertaking. Interscope head, Jimmy Iovine, sensing the potential for another chart topper, pushed the singer to collaborate with multiple musicians and producers. Over the next several months, Stefani brainstormed and wrote songs with Linda Perry, Dallas Austin, Pharrel Williams, the Neptunes, Jimmy Jam, Terry Lewis, Andre 3000, Dr. Dre, Eve, and, for the first time, husband Gavin Rossdale.

"But the goal wasn't to get everybody on my record," she told Ben Wener in an interview for the November 23, 2004 issue of the *Orange County Register.*. "The goal was to make a record that had that feeling I got when I'd go dancing at Studio K at Knott's Berry Farm. You don't feel that anymore. . .I wanted to make a record where every song sounds like a single," Stefani said, "and every single would be someone's guilty pleasure, even if they hate me."

Despite her years of writing and collaborating with Dumont, Kanal, and Young, and No Doubt's work with other musicians on *Rock Steady,* Stefani was very intimidated by the prospect of pairing up with outsiders for this project.

"I think every record No Doubt's made had its own challenges," she told Billy Rainey and Jennifer Vineyard in an interview for MTV. "But this one, for me, was the hardest. When you've never really written with other people, you're exposing yourself, taking your clothes off, saying, 'All right, here we go, this is me, this is you.' And then there's the whole fan thing going on, when you're a fan of the person you're working with. It's humiliating and intimidating even if they're sweet and excited, because you're drowning in their creativity."

She had her first session with Linda Perry, the former lead singer of 4 Non Blondes who has since written and produced hits such as "Get the Party Started" for Pink and Christina Aguilera's "Beautiful." Stefani says that she was so frightened that she cried before heading into the studio. Nevertheless, they wrote a love song their first day. The second day was productive as well—they wrote the song, "What You Waiting For?" which Stefani describes as Perry's challenge to the still-hesitant singer to let loose and start writing. But on the third day, during an attempt at writing a song about the death of a friend, Perry came up with lyrics before Stefani, who got very upset and left.

"It was really inspiring," Stefani told Marc Spitz in the December 2004 issue of *Spin.* "But by the last day of our session, I was really dried out. I had no ideas, and every time I'd leave the room, she'd be writing and I'd be like, "You gotta slow down. You're writing my record!" I was getting pissed off. She's writing these lyrics, and that's when it really crossed the line. It was my insecurities, but I couldn't take it. I was like, 'Call the manager! I need to go home! I need to write on my own.' I told Linda, 'It's nothing against you.' And she was like, 'You are crazy.'"

Perry downplays Stefani's reaction that day. "I think Gwen is very over-critical of herself," Perry told Ariel Levy in an interview for the December 2004 issue of *Blender*. "There was one day where she had a little insecurity breakdown. But I found it very endearing; I loved seeing her that insecure. You meet a lot of people who have half her talent and they think they're God's creative monster."

When she left Perry's studio, Stefani headed straight to her safety zone, her writing partner Kanal. Kanal was able to shake her out of her funk. He'd already written some tracks with her album in mind, and that night they wrote the song "Crash."

Despite the shaky start to their collaboration, Stefani worked with Perry again. She introduced Perry to Dallas Austin during a session. The trio had so much fun that they ended up writing a song, "Danger Zone," in under an hour.

Perry didn't hesitate when Stefani invited her over. "Gwen's just fun," she later told Jin Moon in an interview for the Fall 2003 issue of *Playback Magazine*. "We laugh all day long. We're both kind of nerds. We're geeks. We're stupid. And so we get along well in that way...We have a really good time. I'm very inspired by her, and it's just very light, which is nice."

Perhaps because she'd gotten over the initial trepidation of working with new partners, Stefani fared better in subsequent writing sessions. She still felt insecure, but made a commitment to banish her ego from the process. It was hard to shake entirely. She felt overwhelmed at the outset when she sat down with Andre 3000 of Outkast to write "Bubble Pop Electric."

" I always felt like if I were a boy, I'd definitely be Andre," she told Marc Sptiz in an interview for the December 16, 2004 issue of *Spin*. "He really did bring a lot to the table, and I was trying to keep above water with how talented that guy is. But by the end, it felt like a collaboration."

Luckily for Stefani, she saved the toughest for last. Dr. Dre repeatedly sent her back to the drawing table with songs she'd written. He suggested a track called "Rich Girl," which was based on the "If I Were a Rich Man," song from the musical *Fiddler on the Roof*. He left Stefani and writing partner Eve in charge of updating the lyrics.

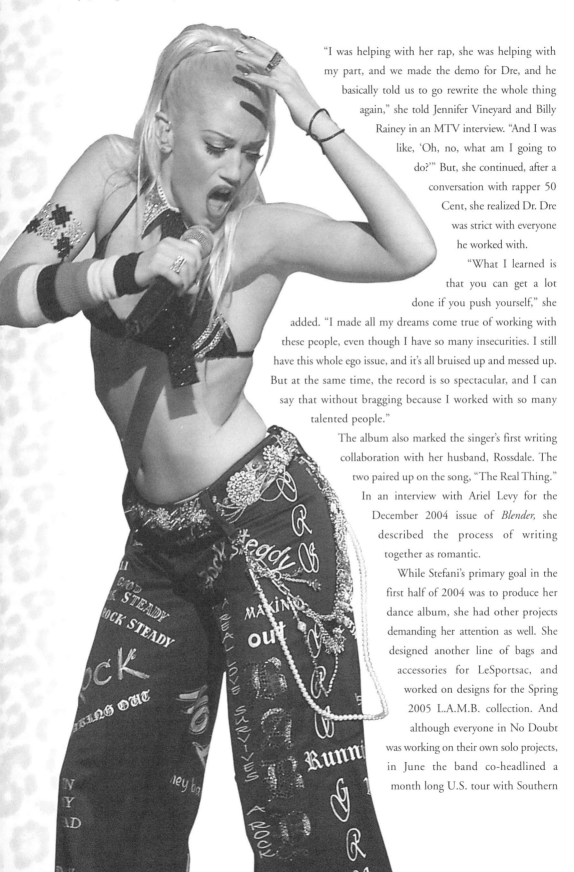

"I was helping with her rap, she was helping with my part, and we made the demo for Dre, and he basically told us to go rewrite the whole thing again," she told Jennifer Vineyard and Billy Rainey in an MTV interview. "And I was like, 'Oh, no, what am I going to do?'" But, she continued, after a conversation with rapper 50 Cent, she realized Dr. Dre was strict with everyone he worked with.

"What I learned is that you can get a lot done if you push yourself," she added. "I made all my dreams come true of working with these people, even though I have so many insecurities. I still have this whole ego issue, and it's all bruised up and messed up. But at the same time, the record is so spectacular, and I can say that without bragging because I worked with so many talented people."

The album also marked the singer's first writing collaboration with her husband, Rossdale. The two paired up on the song, "The Real Thing." In an interview with Ariel Levy for the December 2004 issue of *Blender,* she described the process of writing together as romantic.

While Stefani's primary goal in the first half of 2004 was to produce her dance album, she had other projects demanding her attention as well. She designed another line of bags and accessories for LeSportsac, and worked on designs for the Spring 2005 L.A.M.B. collection. And although everyone in No Doubt was working on their own solo projects, in June the band co-headlined a month long U.S. tour with Southern

California cohorts, Blink-182. At the end of the summer, the band got together again to accept two awards, Best Group Video and Best Pop Video, for "It's My Life" at the MTV Video Music Awards.

In September, Stefani released the first single off *Love.Angel.Music.Baby.*, "What You Waiting For?" The lyrics, written during her initial writing sessions with producer Linda Perry, were their attempts to get the singer past a serious case of writer's block:

You got your million-dollar contract / And they're all waiting for your hot track / What you waiting for / Take a chance you stupid ho.

Despite the lyrics' tongue-in-cheek admonitions and the support of her collaborators at the time, Stefani needed an extra boost to get her creative juices flowing. The Harajuku girls of Tokyo—a subculture of fashion-obsessed women famous for their often-wild style combinations—long a fascination for the trendsetting Stefani, became her muse. "[The Harajuku Girls] became my muses, my inspiration, and my confidence," she told *Flare.com's* Michele Sponagle. "Every time I drew a blank, I dreamed about [my posse]."

In addition to references in several songs on *Love.Angel.Music.Baby.*, Stefani gave them their full due, *Harajuku girls, you got the wicked style,* in their own song, appropriately titled, "Harajuku Girls."

In the video for "What You Waiting For," her muses made the leap from the page onto the screen. They accompanied Stefani, attired in an outfit perhaps best described as a sexed-up Alice, in a wild, frenetic romp through Wonderland that manages to make Tom Petty's psychedelic take on the Mad Hatter's tea party look tame.

The four Harajuku girls became Stefani's posse, popping up in two other *L.A.M.B.* videos and accompanying the singer to public appearances.

After the release of *L.A.M.B.*, on November 23, the inevitable questions arose about whether Stefani was leaving her No Doubt band members for her Harajuku girls and a solo career. She reminded the press that the album was hardly a solo effort given the number of musicians and producers who contributed to it, including No Doubt bassist Kanal. 'Right now I'm all about trying things I've never done," Stefani told Jenny Eliscu in an interview for the January 30, 2005 issue, *The Observer.* 'I'm a woman and I'm thirty-five. I don't have that much time left to do this kind of pop record. Let's be real.'

L.A.M.B. flew off the shelves. Two weeks after it hit stores, it sold half a million copies. Not everyone got the point of the album. In its November 21, 2004 issue, the *New York Daily News'* music reviewer commented, "Nearly every cut channels the dinky rhythms and palm-tree'd production of L.A. pop's worst era...Obviously, Stefani can't help the sonic boo-boos of her youth. The question is: Must she make all of us pay for them?"

Although many reviewers felt compelled to point out that the album was fluff, they also readily acknowledged that they couldn't help but like it. *Rolling Stone* reviewer Rob Sheffield, on the other hand, gave Stefani high marks in his December 9, 2004 review:

"No Doubt singer flies solo and hits the dance floor for her first solo album, Gwen Stefani could have gone the solemn schlock route. But fortunately, she obeys her disco instincts on *Love.Angel.Music.Baby.* It's an irresistible party: Trashy, hedonistic, and deeply weird. Stefani's gum-snapping sass brings out the beast in her beatmasters, especially the Neptunes in "Hollaback Girl" and Andre 3000 in "Bubble Pop Electric."

The second single released off *L.A.M.B.* was the Dr. Dre produced, "Rich Girl." In addition to back-up vocals, Eve contributed a mid-song rap. Stefani seems to be gloating about the wealth she now enjoys (with specific references to her own life) with lines like:

If I were a rich girl.....I'd buy everything / Clean out Vivienne Westwood / In my Galliano gown / No, wouldn't just have one hood / A Hollywood mansion if I could / Please book me first-class to my fancy house in London town.

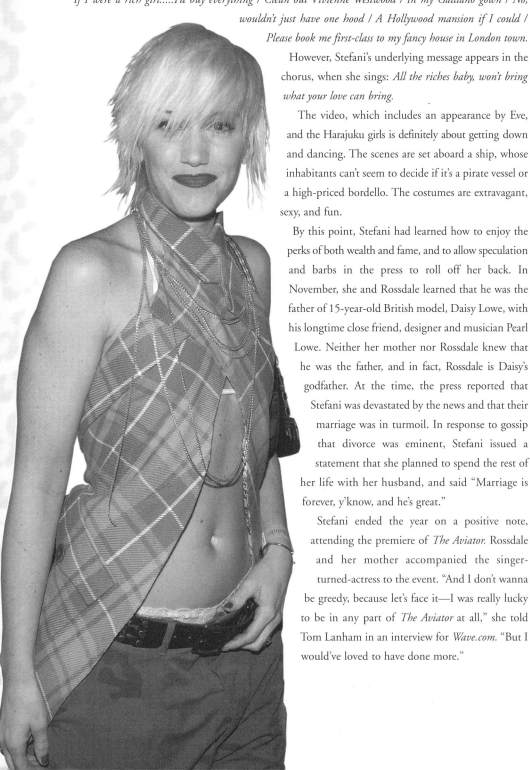

However, Stefani's underlying message appears in the chorus, when she sings: *All the riches baby, won't bring what your love can bring.*

The video, which includes an appearance by Eve, and the Harajuku girls is definitely about getting down and dancing. The scenes are set aboard a ship, whose inhabitants can't seem to decide if it's a pirate vessel or a high-priced bordello. The costumes are extravagant, sexy, and fun.

By this point, Stefani had learned how to enjoy the perks of both wealth and fame, and to allow speculation and barbs in the press to roll off her back. In November, she and Rossdale learned that he was the father of 15-year-old British model, Daisy Lowe, with his longtime close friend, designer and musician Pearl Lowe. Neither her mother nor Rossdale knew that he was the father, and in fact, Rossdale is Daisy's godfather. At the time, the press reported that Stefani was devastated by the news and that their marriage was in turmoil. In response to gossip that divorce was eminent, Stefani issued a statement that she planned to spend the rest of her life with her husband, and said "Marriage is forever, y'know, and he's great."

Stefani ended the year on a positive note, attending the premiere of *The Aviator*. Rossdale and her mother accompanied the singer-turned-actress to the event. "And I don't wanna be greedy, because let's face it—I was really lucky to be in any part of *The Aviator* at all," she told Tom Lanham in an interview for *Wave.com*. "But I would've loved to have done more."

CHAPTER FIFTEEN

𝔓latinum 𝔅londe 𝔏ife

G iven the rave reviews she got from Scorsese and fellow cast members, it's very likely that
Stefani will get more offers in the future—if she has time to fit them in, that is. So far 2005,
has seen the continued success of all things L.A.M.B.

She performed at the Grammy's and had been nominated for two awards, Best Female Pop Vocal for
"What You Waiting For" and, with No Doubt, for Best Pop Performance by a Duo or Group for "It's
My Life."

Stefani is already working on designs for her 2006 collection, and has added a line of sneakers to her
offerings. She launched Harajuku Lovers, a creative twist on the standard rock merchandise line. In
addition to the traditional tanks and t-shirts, she'll be designing sweats, stationery, accessories, bags, and
housewares. In partnership with Hewlett Packard, Stefani also designed her first gadget, the HP
Photosmart R607 Harajuku Lovers Digital Camera.

In the U.S., Love.Angel.Music.Baby." surpassed Platinum in less than six months after its November
23, 2004 launch. The album reached #5 on the *Billboard 200* and as of July 2005, was still holding
steady in the Top 15 albums. This summer saw the release of two more singles off
Love.Angel.Music.Baby., the Pharrel Williams produced "Hollaback Girl" and "Cool," which was written
by Dallas Austin.

"Hollaback Girl" is a hybrid of hip hop and marching band, and is Stefani's attitude song, as she described it in an interview with Lauren Gitlin for the June 7, 2005 issue of *Rolling Stone*. "I did the whole record, but I knew I didn't have my attitude song—my 'this is my history, you can't erase it song," said Stefani." I knew I wanted a song like that."

The video mirrors the "high school" tone of the lyrics, *So that's right dude, meet me at the bleachers / No principals, no student-teachers.* Filmed at a southern California high school, it features Gwen and her Harajuku Girls, driving up in a banana yellow convertible, in full-on gangsta fashion. They also appear as cheerleaders and members of the marching band. At

press time, "Hollaback Girl" had been nominated for four MTV Video Awards, for Video of the Year, Best Female Video, Best Pop Video, and Best Choreography. Stefani was also in the running for two awards for "What You Waiting For?" for Best Art Direction and Best Editing.

New wave ballad single "Cool" is the fourth single off the album. Producer Dallas Austin had originally written the music tracks after hearing "Don't Speak," and in response to his break up with a girlfriend, with whom he'd remained friends, but set them aside for several years because he wasn't sure what to do with them. The lyrics Stefani wrote for "Cool" were about her current relationship with Tony Kanal, and how happy she was that they managed to remain friends. *And after all the obstacles / It's good to see you now with someone else / And it's such a miracle that you and me are still good friends / After all that we've been through / I know we're cool.*

Long-time No Doubt collaborator Sophie Muller directed the video, ironically, she also directed the video for "Don't Speak." In the video, Kanal plays Stefani's ex, visiting with a new wife. The scenes alternate between the three having tea and memories of the two former lovers.

With "Cool" Stefani comes full circle with her subject matter. In an interview with Christian Wright for *Allure* magazine in 2003, Stefani reflected on the circumstances that landed her where she is today. "I didn't want to break up with Tony," she said. "But it was the best thing that ever happened to me. Because I found my gift, which I think is songwriting. It gave me a life, it gave me a personality, it gave me everything I have. He got the lifestyle he wanted, the whole wild band life. And I got to find Gavin, someone who really cares about me. And the one thing I feel blessed about, and both of us feel this way, is that our friendship remained. I mean how rare is that?"

As of press time, the friends and writing partners were working on Stefani's follow up to *Love.Angel.Music.Baby.* The singer's collaborations had produced more songs than could fit on the first album. Stefani will be taking some of those tracks, along with new compositions written with Kanal and Pharell Williams, among others. The album is due out at the end of 2005.

With opening act Black Eyed Peas, Stefani is slated to tour in support of *Love.Angel.Music.Baby.* from mid-October through November, which will leave her with just enough time for a little rest and relaxation before she heads back into the studio with bandmates Dumont, Kanal, and Young to start work on the next No Doubt album. Beyond that, Stefani isn't sure about what the future holds. "At a certain point I'm going to want to have a family,' she told Jenny Eliscu in an interview for *The Observer* for the January 30, 2005 issue, "and I'm not going to have time to be running around the world doing this and being greedy.

"I can always write songs. But can I always wear an Alice-in-Wonderland costume? I probably shouldn't...I've been making a conscious effort not to think about the future. I'm lucky to not have a real job, to be able to express myself, be creative, and be relevant."

Whatever path Stefani chooses to follow, whether it's to continue creating music, pursue her design career, conquer Hollywood, start a family, or something entirely different, she'll rock.

Discography

EPs

No Doubt: Live in L.A.
Intro (Star Wars - live)

Spiderwebs (live)

Just A Girl (live)

Excuse Me Mr. (live)

Open The Gate

Trauma/Interscope Records, 1995

Full Length

No Doubt
BND
Let's Get Back
Ache
Get On The Ball
Move On
Sad For Me
Doormat
Big City Train
Trapped In A Box
Sometimes
Sinking
A Little Something Refreshing
Paulina
Brand New Day
Interscope/Atlantic Records, 1992

Tragic Kingdom
Spiderwebs
Excuse Me Mr.
Just A Girl
Happy Now?
Different People
Hey You
The Climb
Sixteen
Sunday Morning
Don't Speak
You Can Do It
World Go 'Round
End It On This
Tragic Kingdom
Trauma/Interscope Records, 1995

Beacon Street Collection
Open The Gate
Blue In The Face
Total Hate '95
Stricken
Greener Pastures
By The Way
Snakes
That's Just Me
Squeal
Doghouse
Sea Creature/Interscope Records, 1995
(No Doubt originally released *Beacon Street Collection* as a bootleg in 1995, Interscope re-issued the album in 1997.)

Return of Saturn

Ex-Girlfriend
Simple Kind Of Life
Bathwater
Six Feet Under
Magic's In The Makeup
Artificial Sweetener
Marry Me
New
Too Late
Comforting Lie
Suspension Without Suspense
Staring Problem
Home Now
Dark Blue
Interscope Records, 2000

No Doubt: The Singles 1992-2003

Just A Girl
It's My Life
Hey Baby featuring Bounty Killer
Bathwater
Sunday Morning
Hella Good
New
Underneath It All featuring Lady Saw
Excuse Me Mr.
Running
Spiderwebs
Simple Kind of Life
Don't Speak
Ex-Girlfriend
Trapped In A Box
Interscope Records, 2003

Rock Steady

Rock Steady (Intro)
Hella Good
Hey Baby
Making Out
Underneath It All
Detective
Don't Let Me Down
Start the Fire
Running
In My Head
Platinum Blonde Life
Waiting Room
Rock Steady
Rock Steady Bio
Interscope Records, 2001

Love, Angel, Music, Baby

What You Waiting For?
Rich Girl
Hollaback Girl
Cool
Bubble Pop Electric
Luxurious
Harajuku Girls
Crash
The Real Thing
Serious
Danger Zone
Long Way to Go
Interscope Records, 2004